Hou

Key Point
Basic concepts in point form.

Close Up
Additional hints, notes, tips or background information.

Watch Out!
Areas where problems frequently occur.

Quick Tip
Concise ideas to help you learn what you need to know.

Remember This!
Essential material for mastery of the topic.

COLES NOTES

Moms and Dads' Guide to...

Music Lessons for Kids

Choosing an instrument

When to start lessons

Private lessons and group programs

─────────── ABOUT COLES NOTES ───────────

COLES NOTES have been an indispensable aid to students on five continents since 1948.

COLES NOTES now offer titles on a wide range of general interest topics as well as traditional academic subject areas and individual literary works. All COLES NOTES are written by experts in their fields and reviewed for accuracy by independent authorities and the Coles Editorial Board.

COLES NOTES provide clear, concise explanations of their subject areas. Proper use of COLES NOTES will result in a broader understanding of the topic being studied. For academic subjects, COLES NOTES are an invaluable aid for study, review and exam preparation. For literary works, COLES NOTES provide interesting interpretations and evaluations which supplement the text but are not intended as a substitute for reading the text itself. Use of the NOTES will serve not only to clarify the material being studied, but should enhance the reader's enjoyment of the topic.

© Copyright 1999 and Published by
COLES PUBLISHING. A division of Prospero Books.
Toronto – Canada

Cataloguing in Publication Data
Ehrlich, Tim 1956–
Moms and dads' guide to ... music lessons for kids:
choosing an instrument, when to start lessons,
private lessons and group programs

(Coles notes) ISBN 0-7740-0581-5
1. Music – Instruction and study. 2. Music – Instruction and study – Juvenile.
3. School music – Instruction and study. I. Title. II. Series.

MT740.E33 1999   780'.71   C99-931476-9

Publisher: Nigel Berrisford
Editor: Paul Kropp Communications
Writer: Tim Ehrlich

Book design: Karen Petherick
Layout and illustration: Christine Cullen

Printed and bound in Canada by Webcom Limited
Cover finish : Webcom's Exclusive DURACOAT

Contents

Chapter 1	**Introduction**	1
Chapter 2	**Types of music programs**	3
	Orff	
	Dalcroze	
	Kodály	
	Suzuki	
	Royal Conservatory of Music (RCM)	
Chapter 3	**Choosing an instrument**	10
	Woodwinds	
	Brass	
	Strings	
	Guitars	
	Pianos and keyboards	
	Percussion	
Chapter 4	**Preschool music**	28
	When to begin?	
	Kindermusik	
	Music for young children	
	Other programs	
Chapter 5	**Lessons**	32
	Group lessons	
	Private lessons	
	How to choose a teacher	
	Arranging lessons	
	Talent	
	Recitals and competitions	
Chapter 6	**School music**	40
	Music curriculum	
	High school	
	University and beyond	

Chapter 7	**Choirs and church music** *Community choirs* *Barbershop groups*	44
Chapter 8	**Future careers in music** *Performing* *Teaching* *Church music* *Pop music* *Music retail* *The music business*	47
Chapter 9	**Supporting your child in music** *Practice* *How you can help* *Dealing with frustration* *Motivation* *When your child wants to quit* *Music in the home* *Concerts*	53
Chapter 10	**The language of music**	65
Chapter 11	**Appreciating music** *Classical to modern* *Discography* *Popular music* *Music mania* *Movies about music*	71
Appendix	**Organizations**	84

CHAPTER ONE

Introduction

Since the dawn of civilization humans have been fascinated by music. Even small children will hum, whistle or tap out a beat. Music has sometimes been called the universal language. Although it cannot properly be called a language, it is an acquired form of expression that can enhance our children's ability to communicate both ideas and emotions. Although music varies from country to country and culture to culture, all peoples use music in some form. In that respect it is universal.

Why should our children study music?

More than 2,000 years ago the Greeks regarded music as one of the branches of science. Since music involves both verbal (left brain) and non-verbal (right brain) processes, it exercises the whole mind. Early musical training may well develop brain areas involved in complex mathematics, sculpting and navigation. Results from a 1994 study at the University of California at Irvine seem to bear this out. Children aged three to five were asked to complete a series of five spatial reasoning tasks at the beginning, middle and end of an eight-month period. One group was given musical instruction while the other was given computer instruction. After four months, the group that was given musical training had improved dramatically. A follow-up study on children of kindergarten age, released in 1997, confirmed these results and showed that musical instruction improved reasoning skills more than computer instruction.

In 1996, Martin Gardiner of Brown University in Providence, Rhode Island, showed that grade 1 students improved their reading and math skills when they got regular music and art training too.

At a time when there is an increased emphasis on math and science, music and other artistic subjects are under more budgetary pressure than ever. They are deemed to be frill subjects, but are not frills at all. The school curriculum is designed to educate the whole child. Learning consists of more than simple acquisition and regurgitation of facts and formulas. A vital part of learning and mental development is creativity. Music is one of the best ways to stimulate and develop this.

There are other reasons for studying music. Children learn valuable skills like pattern recognition. Music is often used in conjunction with beginning language skills to teach the concepts of rhyming words and sounds, how syllables work and even spelling rules. Music can add enjoyment to any learning experience.

Music also instills an appreciation of beauty and it can provide an important outlet for self-expression. Since it requires constant practise to learn and improve, music teaches discipline and patience. It requires discipline on the part of parents as well. You will be a partner in your child's musical education whether you realize it or not.

Five good reasons for kids to learn music

1. Music is something beautiful that can be shared.
2. It is something that can be done throughout a lifetime.
3. Music helps instill a sense of discipline.
4. Musical friends can become long-lasting ones.
5. Music helps improve abilities in math and spatial reasoning.

CHAPTER TWO

Types of programs

When you first begin looking at musical instruction for your young child, you are likely to hear a number of baffling names and terms such as Orff, Kodály, Suzuki and eurhythmics. These are well-established teaching approaches that are used by many music instructors.

ORFF (AGE 6-10)

The Orff approach to teaching music was introduced to Canada in the 1960s by the Royal Conservatory of Music. Carl Orff (1895-1982) was a German composer who founded Schulwerk, or Music for Children, with the concept that speech, movement and music are unified. He called this elemental music. The Orff method is based on the things children like to do: sing, chant rhymes, clap, dance and tap a beat on anything near at hand.

In Orff music, children actively participate in the making of music. They are encouraged to hear and make music first and then read and write musical notation later. This is the way we all learned our language skills, so it seems very natural for children. Body sounds and gestures are used for rhythm and the voice is regarded as the first and most natural of instruments. Many of us are used to seeing basic rhythm instruments such as sticks, blocks, drums and other noisemakers used in schools. Along with specially designed glockenspiels and xylophones, these are often referred to as Orff instruments. They allow the child to produce a good musical sound immediately.

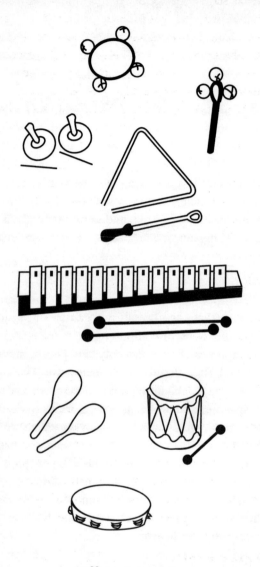

Orff instruments

The Orff approach, as practised in North America, uses four developmental stages: imitation, exploration, literacy and improvisation. Imitation may be simultaneous or echo-like. The instructor may clap or chant a rhythm, which the students duplicate either with voice, movement or the Orff instruments. Exploration involves the students looking at how they can apply this new information in different ways. For example, they may see what happens when the rhythm is played faster/slower, louder/softer or on a different instrument. The literacy stage introduces both graphic and conventional staff notation. In addition to learning various musical terms, children also learn "secret" words such as drone (a sustained chord), ostinati (repeating pattern) and pentatonic (five-note scale). Secret, in this case, imparts a kind of special nature to the words – the kids only use them for their music. Improvisation is the ultimate stage, with the students applying their learned skills in the creation of their own music.

DALCROZE (AGE 3-7)

Émile Jacques-Dalcroze (1865-1950) devised a system of rhythmic education that he called eurhythmics. Jacques-Dalcroze proposed that the source of musical rhythm was in the body. He noticed that in some of his advanced students there were distinct gaps in their musical abilities. Flaws in rhythm, pitch and intonation demonstrated that mechanical learning was taking place rather than true musical understanding. According to Jacques-Dalcroze, people become musical when the ear, brain and body work as an ensemble. In classes that use Jacques-Dalcroze's approach, children move with the music in order to develop a personal response in following the tempo, rhythm and meter of music.

Although now more closely associated with dance, many music schools use eurhythmics as part of their program, in conjunction with other methods.

KODÁLY (AGE 5-12)

Zoltán Kodály (pronounced Koh-dye) was a Hungarian composer (1882-1967) and a strong advocate of musical education for children. He believed that music belonged to everyone and not just a talented few. The Kodály method insists that music instruction begin early with rhythm training and singing of children's folk songs. This leads gradually to the development of musically independent students who can read and write music with ease.

Instruction often begins with the chanting of syllables such as ta-ti-ti to help the children master the concepts of rhythm in their singing. Kodály also developed a series of hand signs representing the familiar do-re-mi-fa-sol-la-ti-do teaching syllables. The hand signs are used in tandem with singing to reinforce the relationship of tone to rhythm. The most important aspect of the Kodály system is its emphasis on songs. Music comes first, followed by understanding. Children learn by rote, then by note.

SUZUKI (AGE 3-16)

While studying music in Germany during the 1930s, Shinichi Suzuki observed that children did not grow up fluent in their native language. All children have to learn the correct way to speak. He came to believe that music could be learned in the same way children learn to speak and read and write. Although Suzuki's method was developed for the violin, Haruko Kataoka adapted the method and philosophies to create a Suzuki Piano School as well.

The Suzuki method begins with rote learning of songs and strongly emphasizes things such as good tone, proper phrasing and expression. Unencumbered with the demands of reading music, the student is free to concentrate on tone and technique. Even after note reading has started, students are encouraged to play without music.

Suzuki believed that the ability of the young student to manipulate the instrument is crucial. This has given rise to the production of smaller-scale stringed instruments, sometimes referred to as Suzuki violins. In addition to violins, violas and cellos, there are smaller-scale harps as well as a flute with a curved head joint that can accommodate smaller arms.

Strong parental involvement is also an important part of the Suzuki method. Initially parents come to the lessons and practise with the children. Even after a few years, parents should be available to listen and offer help when needed.

It is important to remember that children are different in temperament and dexterity. One of the important factors when considering music lessons is your child's attention span. Children under age six usually do not have the attention span required to benefit from formal instruction or to practise effectively. In addition, a certain physical size and level of co-ordination are required. You are the best judge of your child's limitations. There are some four- or five-year-olds who can handle formal lessons, whereas others may have to wait until eight or nine before beginning. Exposure to music, however, is appropriate at any age.

ROYAL CONSERVATORY OF MUSIC (RCM)

Many music teachers and programs have adopted programs set out by the Royal Conservatory of Music, based in Toronto. The RCM was established in 1886 and has a long tradition of excellence that ranks it among the top musical schools in the world. Alumni include some of Canada's greatest musicians, such as Glenn Gould, John Vickers, Teresa Stratas and Mario Bernardi. The RCM has now expanded internationally with examinations and accredited teachers in the United States and other countries around the globe. This growth is due, in large measure, to its reputation for excellence in performance and education.

RCM programming covers all ages from six months to adult and every level from beginning to professional. There are currently 38 programs available for children and teens and 61 for adults, covering 18 instruments as well as voice and music theory.

For each program (for example, piano) there is a syllabus that outlines a course of study progressing through various levels or grades. These are not analogous to school grades; however, as we shall see further on, high-school credit can be given upon completion of certain levels of RCM examinations. The piano program goes from grades 1 through 10. Students must pass an examination in order to achieve the next grade level. These examinations consist of being able to play a set number of pieces chosen by the student from approved studies' albums. In addition, students must demonstrate technical skills such as scales, arpeggios and triads and take an ear test where they must identify intervals or play back a melody played once by the examiner. All grades also have a sight-reading requirement. All pieces of music and technical skills must be played from memory. This may seem pretty daunting but the various requirements will be thoroughly practised by the time your child is ready to take the examination.

The pupils study and practise from a variety of books and other materials available for each instrument. Using piano as an example, there are four series of studies: repertoire albums, studies albums, student guides and recordings. The repertoire and studies albums are the most commonly used. A typical repertoire album consists of a selection of pieces divided into three to five lists. These pieces are often written by well-known classical and Canadian composers. The books are published by Frederick Harris Music Co. Ltd. and are available at most music stores for under $10. They can also be purchased through your music teacher or music school. If you have a neighbor or relative who has just completed a grade level, you may also be able to borrow the books or purchase them at a nominal cost.

High-school accreditation

As mentioned previously, high-school credit in music can be obtained for completion of certain (RCM) grade levels. If you and your child wish to take advantage of this, it is important to remember:

1. Consultation with the school guidance counsellor for specific details is advised.
2. Accreditation policies are the jurisdiction of each province and can vary. Questions should be directed to your local board of education or high school.

A couple of examples of the type of equivalency that may be granted: In Alberta, credit for grade 11 music can be given for successful completion of grade 7 practical and grade 2 theory in either voice, piano, strings, accordion or guitar. In Ontario, one non-OAC credit will be given for successful completion of grade 8 practical in any musical instrument or voice and grade 2 theory.

Here is an example of the examination requirements for grade 3 piano:

1. **Play three pieces**, one each from Lists A, B and C and two grade 3 studies from the (RCM) grades 3 and 4 studies album.
2. **Technical Test** (Major keys F, B flat, A and Minor keys A, D and G)
- Scales listed above at metronome mark (MM) 92, two octaves, eighth notes, hands separately. Minor scales in both harmonic and melodic forms. C major scale at MM 80 with both hands playing a formula pattern.
- Triads listed above, solid in quarter notes, broken in eighth notes. MM 132 for solid triads and MM 72 for broken triads.
3. **Ear Test**
- Rhythm: To sing, clap or tap the rhythm of a short melody after it has been played twice by the examiner.
- Intervals: (Above – major 3rd, perfect 5th, octave. Below – minor 3rd, perfect 5th. To sing or hum any of the above intervals after the first note has been played once by the examiner.
- Melody Playback: To play back a five-note melody based on the first five notes of a scale that may contain a skip of a third and/or fifth after the examiner has named the key, played the tonic triad once, played the melody twice.
4. **Sight Reading**
- To play a simple short melody in 4/4 time using both hands in the keys of D or G major with the right hand in quarter or half notes and the left hand in half notes.
- To clap or tap a rhythmic pattern in 3/4 time with half, quarter and eighth notes.

CHAPTER THREE

Choosing an instrument

One day your child runs in the house in a rush of excitement declaring, "Mom, Dad, I wanna play the tuba!" To avoid disappointing your child or getting into something you may regret later, it's a good idea to find out what choices are available in instruments and musical instruction and what is suitable for your child's age.

WOODWINDS

Let's begin by looking at the woodwinds. All wind instruments make sound in the same manner — a column of air is made to vibrate and the pitch is changed by either lengthening or shortening this column of air. The woodwinds are so named because they were originally made of wood tubes. Today, oboes, clarinets and recorders are still made of wood or plastic, but flutes are made of metal. Sound is produced either by blowing across an opening as in a flute, or by blowing into a mouthpiece with a vibrating reed. The tube is lengthened or shortened by covering holes or pressing keys along the length of the tube.

The most common instruments in the woodwind family include the recorder, flute, clarinet, oboe, saxophone and bassoon. These are the ones you are most likely to see in a school band. There are others, such the English horn, piccolo, and contrabassoon, but these are really for more advanced musicians. In addition there are a number of miscellaneous instruments such as fifes, tonettes and penny whistles that are also woodwinds. The flute, oboe and clarinet are higher-pitched, or treble, instruments. The bassoon has a low, or bass, sound. The saxophones and recorders range from middle to high.

English horn

Woodwinds

Oboe

Bass clarinet

Clarinet

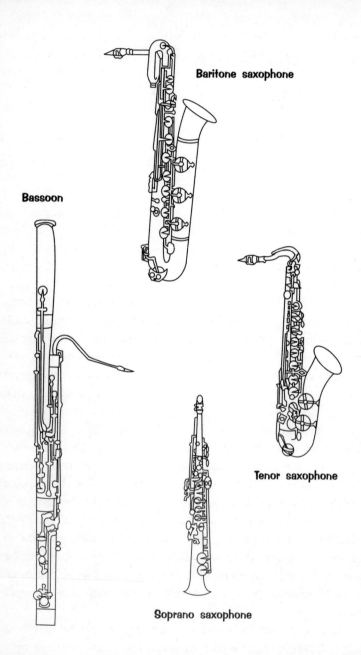

Flute

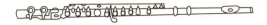

Piccolo

Most children (and adults, too, for that matter) want to see quick results. They want to be able to make a pleasant sound and to be able to play a few simple tunes in a few weeks. The flute, clarinet and recorder are usually good choices because they can give these kinds of results. The oboe and bassoon are more difficult to learn and progress can be slow. (The sound of someone learning to play the oboe has been likened to listening to a person torturing a crow!) Children are less likely to choose the oboe and bassoon, and this may not be so bad since these two are also fairly expensive instruments. Saxophones are very similar to clarinets in playability and children are often attracted to them. They are, however, somewhat large and more suited to older children.

Flute Young children are attracted to the flute by its beautiful sound and may want to begin playing it long before their bodies are ready. Their arms must be long enough to hold the flute in a horizontal position. If your child's arms are too short, the flute will be held at an angle, causing her neck to be crooked in order to have the lips in the proper blowing position. Music should not be a pain in the neck! As mentioned previously, there is a flute available with a crooked head joint to alleviate this problem for younger players.

Because a flute has no reed to produce sound, the shape of the lips is important. Lips that are too thick or too thin can be a handicap. Large front teeth can also be a problem. Your child should not be daunted by all the keys and hardware running along an instrument. There is a golden rule of instruments that says the more complicated they look as machines, the easier they are to play. This is because the hardware does much of the work in changing keys and notes. In contrast, the simple-looking violin requires the player to do all the work.

Clarinet Although the clarinet may seem similar to the recorder, it is different in almost every respect. Recorders are blown like a whistle, whereas the clarinet mouthpiece is held with the front teeth while air is forced past a reed, which vibrates to produce the sound. This is similar to blowing on a blade of grass stretched across two thumbs. There is a pronounced vibration in the mouth, which takes some getting used to.

The clarinet is a very versatile instrument capable of a great range of sound. It is easy to produce a *big* sound with little effort, a fact that cannot be ignored by most parents of novice players. Perhaps it this quality that attracts many boys to the clarinet. Also, just as the flute is closer to the vocal register of girls, the clarinet is closer to that of boys.

In terms of physical suitability, large strong front teeth can be helpful in playing the clarinet. It is also important that your child's fingers be long enough to span the distance between the keys. The pads of the fingertips must be broad enough to cover the open-hole keys.

Saxophone Because the saxophone is not usually regarded as a classical instrument, it is sometimes overlooked by parents. The saxophone is, however, widely employed in concert and marching bands and used extensively in popular music. Of all the musical instruments, the saxophone comes closest to imitating the sound quality of the human voice.

There are four sizes and registers of saxophones: soprano, alto, tenor and baritone. The fingering, as in the flute, is very similar to the recorder and many students can play both the sax and the flute. The sound is produced by a reed in the same manner as the clarinet. There are no great finger stretches but the hands are held out of eyesight and some degree of co-ordination is required. The fact that saxophones are fairly heavy makes them more suitable for children over 12. They are held by a sling that goes around the neck. Saxophones are usually twice as expensive as the flute or clarinet should you choose to buy one.

Oboe and bassoon These two instruments are definitely not for everybody. In the hands of a skilled player, they sound exquisite. In the hands of a beginner they sound, well, excruciating. The sound for both is produced by a double reed, which requires the lips to be folded over the teeth when blowing. It is difficult to force air between this aperture and the resulting back pressure can cause headaches in even a healthy teenager. Breath control is essential and a frail child will have considerable difficulty mastering the techniques. While these instruments are sometimes encouraged by teachers anxious to complete an orchestra, their difficulty makes them suitable only for the most gifted or dedicated students.

In many cases, the size of the instrument may dictate its suitability for your child. Obviously, a tuba is too large for a seven-year-old and the trombone requires arms long enough to extend the slide. Fingers must be large enough to cover holes and reach keys or valves. For wind instruments, younger children might start out on the recorder, which comes in a variety of sizes. Learning to play the recorder is sound training for *any* musical instrument. Of the common musical instruments, only the guitar, violin and cello are produced in smaller sizes for use by very young children.

Recorder The simplest woodwinds of all and by far the most accessible, recorders come in a variety of sizes from the soprano, which sounds like a piccolo, up to the bass, which resembles a bassoon in shape and sounds rather like a clarinet. The smaller sizes are quite suitable for children as young as five years old. While it appears deceptively simple, the recorder is a real instrument and not a toy. In fact, advanced recorder techniques can be quite difficult to master. But even young children can quickly learn to play a simple tune such as "Hot Cross Buns". Pleasing results can come quickly.

BRASS

Like the woodwinds, the brasses are wind instruments. Sound is produced by pursing the lips against the mouthpiece and blowing a raspberry sound. The different notes are produced by changing the shape of the lips or changing the length of tube. The latter change is done with a sliding mechanism as in the trombone, or by means of valves as in the trumpet or tuba.

Trumpet The highest voice in the brass family. It is a powerful, aggressive-sounding instrument often associated with marching and military music. It takes a fair amount of energy to play. The trumpet is a fairly light instrument, so there are no real physical requirements other than your child's hands being large enough to reach and depress all three valves. Your child must also have enough lung power to blow that raspberry sound through the relatively small mouthpiece. The **cornet** is very similar to the trumpet in shape and size but produces a gentler sound and is not quite as much work to play. A **bugle** is similar to the cornet but without valves and therefore has a more limited range of notes.

Trombone The tenor voice to the trumpet's soprano, the trombone is different from other brass instruments in that it does not have valves to control the sound. The pitch is changed by lengthening or shortening the column of air by manually sliding the tube. A trombone looks like a paper clip with a horn at the end. Indeed, the French word for paper clip is *trombone*. The arms of your child must be long enough to extend the slide fully to make all the notes. A good sense of pitch is required because the player is completely in control of the tone.

French horn Also called simply the "horn". It has a mellow and lyrical sound but it can be a very difficult instrument to learn. The mouthpiece is quite small, requiring extremely good lip control. It also takes some effort to blow due to back pressure. This can cause headaches in some children. The **euphonium** covers almost the same range of notes as the French horn and is much easier to play due to its larger mouthpiece. It looks like a very small tuba and is often used in bands, whereas the French horn is almost exclusively an orchestral instrument. French horns are typically expensive as well.

Tuba The gruff bass voice of the brass family. The tuba's mouthpiece is quite large, but it actually takes less energy to play than the trumpet. This is because the tuba acts as an amplifier and does not have to be filled with air. The main drawbacks are carrying it, transporting it and finding a place to put it. A tuba won't fit under your child's bed.

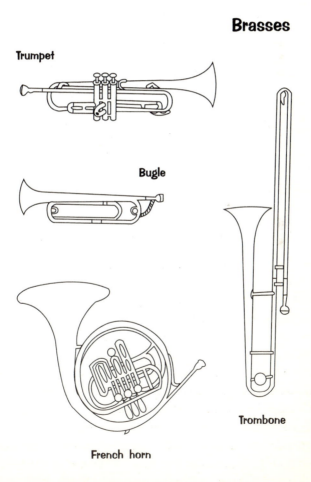

Brasses

Trumpet

Bugle

Trombone

French horn

Sousaphone

Baritone horn

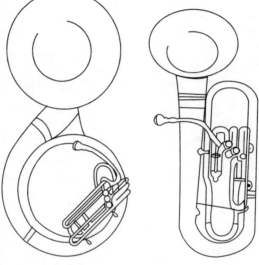

Flügelhorn

STRINGS

There are two distinctly different categories of string. These are the bowed or orchestral instruments such as the violin, and the plucked instruments such as the guitar and banjo.

Most children's exposure to bowed instruments begins at school by around 11 or 12. Private lessons often begin as early as seven, although instructors using the Suzuki method may begin children as early as three or four.

The strings are one of the simplest groups of instruments and, paradoxically, the most difficult to play well. This is because there are no mechanical keys, valves or other aids used to produce the sound. The musician is solely responsible for the sound, and a string player must have a good sense of pitch. If your child is going to begin playing a stringed instrument, be prepared for many sour notes and unusual sounds in the beginning years. Once the technique improves, however, the sound is sublime.

Violin Since the violin is the soprano voice of the strings, it most often plays the melody lines in an orchestra. It comes in a number of sizes some as small as one-sixteenth size, which can enable children as young as three or four to begin learning. The violin is nestled under the chin, often supported by a sponge, against the neck and shoulder. The left hand does not actually support the instrument but is free to make the notes on the finger board. A slightly curved bow strung with horsehair is drawn across the strings causing them to vibrate. A substance called rosin is rubbed on the bow to enable it to better grip the strings.

Viola As the alto voice, the viola rarely plays the melody and is more suited to a student who is prepared to remain in the background. It is larger than the violin and thus is better suited for older children and their larger hands.

Cello is the tenor voice, and will also play melody. It is a larger instrument held between the knees and balanced on a peg protruding from the bottom of the instrument. Of the string instruments, the cello comes closest to the human voice in tone.

Strings

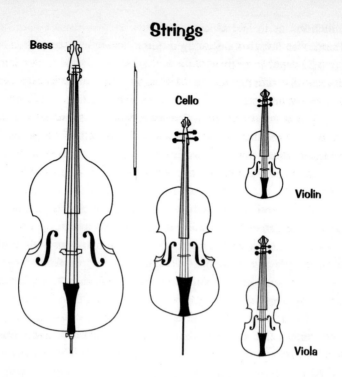

Double bass is the largest of the strings. It is played with the musician standing or seated on a stool. As with all the orchestral strings, it is played either by bowing or plucking. The bass is also a popular instrument in modern forms of music, such as jazz. Older children are more likely to be attracted to the larger size of the bass, which is good because it takes larger hands and arms to reach the notes along the neck.

Guitar A very popular instrument for kids to learn. There is a tendency to want to emulate performers they hear and see on radio or television and many children begin playing on their own using books or just by experimentation. There also are many fine programs for both the acoustic and electric guitar. One of the reasons for the popularity of the guitar is the abundance of music available for it. In addition, a great deal of popular and rock music is centered around guitar playing.

The typical guitar has six strings of varying pitch, which are stretched along a fingerboard that has metal ridges called frets embedded in it. The fingers press the strings against the frets to change the length of the string while the other hand plucks. The guitar is capable of producing both melody and harmony simultaneously, like the piano, and thus it is a very satisfying instrument to play on its own.

There are three main types of guitar. The **acoustic guitar** has a hollow body with a round sound hole and metal strings that give it a bigger, fuller sound. It is played by picking and strumming with the fingers and thumb, or by using a flat plastic pick that is held between the fingers and thumb.

The **classical guitar** is similar in shape to the acoustic guitar but slightly smaller, with a wider neck, and strings made usually of nylon. It is most often played in a seated position and almost exclusively with the fingers and thumb.

The **electric guitar** usually has a solid body and a slightly narrower neck. The distinguishing characteristic of the electric guitar is the circuitry that enables the player to enhance the sound with an electric amplifier. (Some parents may take issue with the term enhance.)

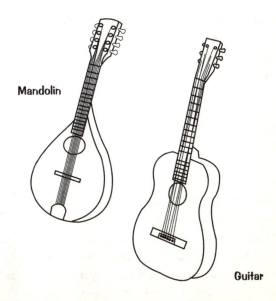

There are a number of other instruments in the string family such as the **banjo**, **mandolin** and **autoharp** but these tend to be very specialized instruments for which very little formal instruction can be found. Most people who take them up are already proficient on another instrument such as the piano or guitar.

PIANOS AND KEYBOARDS

The **piano** is perhaps the most popular instrument of all for beginning music lessons. Even children who take up other instruments will also sometimes learn the piano for enjoyment or to supplement their music studies.

The sound of the piano is produced by a series of strings that cover 7 ⅓ octaves. When one of the 88 keys is pressed, a damper is raised and a hammer strikes one or more strings, causing them to vibrate. The strings are affixed to a large, heavy sound board, which adds resonance. The piano has two, or sometimes three, pedals that have the effect of either softening the sound or allowing the strings to sustain their vibration.

Pianos come primarily in two forms – upright and grand with many sizes of each. The upright has the strings and sound board oriented vertically. This is typically the type of piano most of us would purchase for our home. The grand piano has the strings and sound board mounted horizontally in a sort of kidney shape, and is the type we normally see in concert halls.

A piano needs to be tuned regularly. Most piano tuners recommend once a year. Changes in humidity or moving a piano can put it out of tune. It is a fairly complex instrument and tuning requires a professional. A good piano tuner may charge anywhere from $50 to $100, depending on the time it takes.

One other type of piano that has gained in popularity is the **electric piano**. This instrument looks a little like an organ. It has a long slender body and usually a full set of 88 keys. Electric pianos can sound remarkably similar to acoustic pianos and some of the better models do a passable job of imitating the action, or feel, of the keys. They are easier to move than a regular piano and they do not need to be tuned. Electronic pianos are often used by beginning students whose parents do not want to invest in the more expensive traditional piano.

Electronic organs are also fairly popular, particularly where space is at a premium. Electronic circuitry is used to produce the sound, which mimics that of a pipe organ. There are a variety of types capable of producing many different sounds.

Electronic keyboards, or synthesizers, are designed to be completely portable. They can produce sounds similar to everything from guitars to jet engines and come in sizes ranging from 24 inches to a full 88 keys.

PERCUSSION

When most of us think of percussion we think of drums. And when it comes to kids and drums, we often think of racket and having to make space in the garage. There are very few opportunities for kids to receive school instruction in percussion. Lessons are usually private and are offered for the traditional rock 'n' roll or jazz drum sets.

Percussion, though, involves many different types of instruments. There are two basic types:

- tuned percussion such as the timpani (or kettle drums), xylophones and glockenspiels
- untuned percussion such as the snare drum, tambourine, cymbals and bass drum

Invariably, these are used in orchestras and are studied no earlier than high school or in university by music students.

GETTING A MUSICAL INSTRUMENT FOR YOUR CHILD

School loaners If your child attends a school where there is instruction available for specific instruments, you may be able to borrow the instrument while your child is learning it. This can work out nicely if there are enough instruments to go around. But in times of declining funding for music programs, this may not be the case, and two or more students may have to share. This will require co-operation to arrange practise at home.

Renting Another alternative to buying an instrument is renting. Renting may be the way to go if your child is just trying an instrument for the first time. It would be annoying not to mention expensive to spend $1,500 on a saxophone only to have your child abandon it eight months down the road. Another advantage to renting is that many music stores have plans whereby you can apply a portion of the rental to the purchase price of the instrument if you decide to buy it later on. This is similar to the rent-to-own option used by some appliance dealers.

It is preferable to rent a new instrument at the outset instead of a used one. At the end of the rental period, you could then apply the fee toward the purchase of a new instrument. Let's face it. Your child is also more likely to be enthusiastic about taking up music with a shiny new instrument than with a used one. Another advantage to renting new instruments is the smaller chance of hidden damage or defects. An instrument that is continually out for repair is a source of frustration you can ill afford.

If you are considering one of the instruments that are scaled to size, such as the violin, cello or guitar, renting makes it easy to trade up as the child grows. If you purchase one of these, be sure to inquire about trading up when the time comes.

Another important thing to be clear about is the terms of the rental. Ask about fees for maintenance or service, repair costs and insurance for perils such as theft. It is best to know about this "fine print" to avoid an expensive surprise. If the music store does not offer insurance, then inquire with your own insurance broker. Home policies often include musical instruments up to a certain value and, for more expensive instruments, extra coverage can be arranged.

Buying an instrument can be a daunting experience, especially for someone of limited musical knowledge. One of the easiest places to get advice is, of course, from a music teacher. If your child is ready to take lessons and you have selected an instructor, you may feel comfortable asking for a recommendation. Some instructors will even accompany you to a music store. This may cost you the price of a lesson, but it is well worth the time and money to have someone with experience evaluate the condition and the tone, and the fairness of the price. If you do not have a teacher yet, you may know someone who plays an instrument or has musical knowledge and can give some advice.

Below is a chart showing an approximate price range for new instruments. If you are looking for a used instrument it is a good idea to stick to music stores. It may be tempting to pick up what seems like a good deal at a garage sale or pawn shop, but you can't be sure of the instrument's quality or condition. It should be noted that these costs are only guidelines and are subject to availability and market demand. A good instrument will usually hold its value for a long time and, in some cases, can actually appreciate in value.

Trumpet	$ 620–$1,600
Trombone	$ 660–$2,270
French horn	$ 1,500–$3,000
Flute	$ 525–$1,900
Violin	$ 125–$15,000
Clarinet	$ 460–$2,700
Saxophone	$ 1,000–$3,000
Acoustic guitar	$ 125–$1,700
Electric guitar + amplifier	$ 200–$2,000
Drum set	$ 800–$3,000
Piano*	$ 2,400 and up

CARE AND MAINTENANCE OF INSTRUMENTS

Once your child has an instrument, there is an investment both in money and effort and it must be cared for.

Strings Violins need to be kept in tune. Temperature and humidity affect the tuning and it will need to be adjusted from time to time. Your instructor may take care of this for the child until she is old enough. If you want to do it yourself you can use a piano to get the correct pitches for the strings or, if a piano is not available, you can purchase an inexpensive pitch pipe from a music store.

Violins and violas need to be kept in their cases to prevent dust from getting at them and protect them from accidental bumps and bruises. Larger stringed instruments such as cellos should also be kept in their cases standing up.

From time to time, the bow may have to be restrung or one of the strings on the instrument replaced. This can easily be done at a music store, where you can get advice on the proper replacement strings.

Guitars should be stored in a case if you have one. As with all stringed instruments, guitars need to be kept in tune. Humidity affects the tuning of a guitar and strings stretch over time. The guitar should be checked for tuning each time it is played. This can be done with a piano, if one is available, or by purchasing an inexpensive pitch pipe.

Woodwinds The woodwinds are usually taken apart and stored in a case. After each use, the instrument should be cleaned with a soft cloth and a cleaning rod, which is usually supplied with the instrument. Reed instruments such as the clarinet or oboe use a cane reed. These are fragile and will need to be replaced periodically. A music store can supply you with replacement reeds and it is a good idea to have a couple of spares on hand. Once in a while mechanical woodwinds such as the clarinet or flute may need a tune-up. This involves a careful cleaning and lubricating of all the moving parts. All keys are checked for proper alignment and any pads on the keys that are damaged can be replaced. Tune-ups are done by qualified instrument repair shops and can cost up to $100.

Brass Like the woodwinds, brass instruments have moving parts that need to be cleaned and lubricated. Some parts, such as the valves on a trumpet, are easily taken apart and lubricated with the appropriate oil. Brass instruments have a small valve, usually located in one of the bottom loops, which is called the spit valve. As the musician plays, condensation collects in the tubing and this needs to be drained off. In addition to being unpleasant, the moisture provides a breeding ground for bacteria and mould.

It is a good idea to leave the brass instrument in its case. Not only will this keep it cleaner but, since brass is a soft metal, it is easily dented by accidental bumps and dings.

CHAPTER FOUR

Preschool music

WHEN TO BEGIN?
The sooner you can expose children to music, the more likely they are to be receptive to instruction and develop a strong appreciation. Some programs such as the Suzuki method can begin as early as three, but formal musical instruction usually begins around age six or seven. The reasons for this are threefold. First, there is a certain level of physical development required (hand size, finger strength, lung power, etc.). Second, children younger than six seldom have the attention span to make use of a half-hour private lesson. Third, music lessons require practise, which means discipline. Frankly, music practise will come a poor second to trucks and dolls to the average four-year-old.

You may not be a singer, but even if you need a bucket to carry a tune, your child is not a music critic. She will enjoy your music and your enjoyment of it.

Television, for all its flaws, does provide some good programming that relies heavily on music. A prime example is *Barney and Friends*. Older children and adults regard the purple dinosaur and affected manner of the children on the show with cynicism, but there is a good reason why the two- to five-year-old set idolizes Barney. Every activity involves a short, singable, happy tune. *Sesame Street*, *Sharon, Lois & Bram* and *Eric's World* are other programs that have a strong emphasis on music and are tremendously popular with preschoolers.

Many of us grew up watching Disney cartoons. One characteristic of these classics is a well-written musical score. Part of what makes these films so entertaining is the fact that music makes them a total package.

Music in the womb

Your child's first exposure to music can begin before birth. Studies have shown that human fetuses will move toward the source of sound when music is played. Relaxing, rhythmic music is not only pleasant for you but for your unborn child as well. Humming or whistling along to a tune that makes you happy seems to have a positive effect on the person inside. Even if you are not a classical-music buff, don't ignore the classics. Studies have shown that students in school do better work when classical music is played in the background. This phenomenon is sometimes referred to as the "Mozart effect".

In addition to the many informal ways you can expose your preschooler to music, there are several more structured learning experiences available. Some of the more well-known include: Kindermusik, Music for Young Children, and YMCA or YWCA theme programs.

There are a number of wonderful children's recordings geared especially to toddlers. Here are a few suggestions, all by widely known children's entertainers. These are just representative selections and any recordings by these artists would be appropriate.

- *Singable Songs for the Very Young*, Raffi (1976) Troubadour Records
- *Car Tunes for Summertime*, Sharon, Lois & Bram (1989) Elephant Records
- *Diamonds and Dragons*, Charlotte Diamond (1988) Hug Bug Records
- *A House Is a House for Me*, Fred Penner (1991) Oak Street Music
- *Walt Disney's Songs from Peter Pan* (1982) Walt Disney Music
- *There's a Hippo in My Tub*, Anne Murray (1977) Capitol Records
- *Dream Catcher*, Jack Grunsky (1993) Den Music

- *Mr. Dressup and Jim Parker: Favorite Songs*, Butternut Music
- *Eric's World Record*, Eric Nagler (1994) Tanglewood Records

KINDERMUSIK

Kindermusik means literally "children's music". It began in the former West Germany in the late 1960s and was translated into English in the early '70s and reworked a few years later to add a multicultural perspective. This program was designed by early childhood education specialists for specific age groups and developmental levels from birth to seven years.

In Kindermusik classes, children sing and move, chant, play simple instruments and listen. The emphasis is on process and not performance. Classes are structured but geared toward fun. Individual development is encouraged and group interaction is strengthened. Parents are encouraged to participate in classes and at home with tapes and other materials provided. Kindermusik is a private franchise operation with over 3,000 qualified teachers in North America and 20 other countries.

The types of programming include:

- **Birth to 18 months**–classes include babes in arms, crawlers and toddlers. Classes are made up of eight to 12 children accompanied by parents or caregivers and are typically a half-hour long. Nursery rhymes, colorful books and playful group dancing aid in visual tracking, shape and color recognition and language development.
- **18 months to 3 years**–children moving to music, repeating sounds and making sounds of their own. Simple percussion instruments are introduced, such as those used in the Orff method. Chanting, listening and rhythm are used to encourage creativity and learning. Parents interact with their child.
- **3½ to 5 years**–classes are slightly longer (up to 50 minutes). Parents and siblings are invited during the last 15 minutes of the class to participate. There is more creative movement, listening activities and playing of percussion instruments. Children begin to explore musical concepts such as rhythm, melody and dynamics. Weekly at-home activities may include making a simple instrument or playing a music-related card game.

- **4½ to 7 years**-classes are 60 minutes with the last 10 minutes for parent/sibling participation. This program follows the traditional school year September to May. Some of the more structured elements of music are introduced such as ear training, sight reading, musical notation and appreciation of different musical cultures.
- Some areas may offer a more advanced level for seven to nine year olds. This program expands on the above program but focuses on singing, instruction in recorder and Orff instruments and ensemble playing.

MUSIC FOR YOUNG CHILDREN

This is another fine program founded in 1980 by music educator Francis Balodis. Its main focus is on keyboard learning. Students aged three to eight are given instruction geared toward Conservatory exams. Children progress through three levels of instruction in preparation for the grade one piano examination of the Royal Conservatory of Music. Original music by Canadian composers is often used.

Like Kindermusik, Music for Young Children is a franchise operation that has local programs in most major centers. Check your Yellow Pages or contact the address at the end of this book for further information.

OTHER PROGRAMS

If there is a local YMCA or YWCA in your area, there are usually programs for children from 18 months to five years that emphasize music and movement. The classes are two to three hours in length and may be one, two or three days a week. Though they are not specifically educational, they nonetheless give children an opportunity to experience music in a fun environment. Music is combined with games and activities with fun names like "music maniacs" or "toddler tunes". These programs are low-cost, with a less demanding time commitment. If cost is a problem, many municipalities have fee-assistance programs.

The Royal Conservatory of Music There are two programs that are usually available through most private music schools or academies. Music and Your Baby is for children six to 36 months old, and Preparatory Music is for three to five year olds.

CHAPTER FIVE

Lessons

All right, your child is determined to play the piano, guitar, clarinet or (shudder) drums. Now what? There are a couple of options. While it is true that kids get music in their local school curricula, those in-class lessons are only intended to impart some very basic musical principles. Sadly, it is also a fact that music is declining in importance as school budgets are under increasing pressure to do more with less.

For an adequate musical education, you will probably want to begin private lessons for your child. There is usually a teacher for every instrument you can imagine, including musical theory.

What is musical theory anyway?

Music has very elaborate and well-defined rules for composition and performance. Theory is the study of how all these rules work and come together to produce a great piece of music. Students who study theory learn the principles of harmony, how scales work, how to rewrite music in another key, tempo, dynamics and a whole lot of Italian words for these things. It is important to understand the principles of theory in order to compose, understand and sometimes play music. That being said, lessons in music theory are probably not for beginning students. It is more suitable for kids over 10 years of age with two or three of years of instrumental study under their belts.

Which is better, individual or group lessons? Should they be in a studio or in your home? There are no hard and fast rules. It depends on your circumstances and the type of instrument.

GROUP LESSONS

At first blush, a private lesson may seem to offer better teaching than a group lesson, but there are some instances where a group lesson may be preferable. Sometimes a particular teacher only offers group lessons and that teacher may be the best one for your child. There is also something to be said for the camaraderie that lessons in a group setting can provide.

Group lessons are also frequently less expensive than individual lessons. This can be an important consideration for families on a tight budget. Guitar classes are often conducive to a group setting. Beginning studies in piano, strings, brass, woodwinds and percussion can also be in a group setting. For advanced students, however, individual instruction is a must.

PRIVATE LESSONS

There are many music teachers out there. As in any profession, there are good ones, bad ones and many in-between. So how does one go about locating a good one?

1. There is, of course, the Yellow Pages. You will find some larger studios offering a host of musical choices. They usually have well-developed programs for a variety of instruments as well as voice instruction.
2. Lessons are usually offered by or through music stores. The instructors there are rarely employed by the store itself, but pick up students on a referral basis.
3. Word-of-mouth can be a good way to find an effective teacher. Friends, neighbors, relatives or colleagues at work may be able to recommend someone with whom they are comfortable.
4. If you are a churchgoer, the music or choir director may be able to suggest someone, or perhaps may even give lessons on the side.
5. Library bulletin boards often have cards or flyers for private music lessons.
6. Try newspaper classifieds or local magazine ads. Keep an eye open especially around early September or Christmas for these.

7. If your area has a college or university, there may be a music department. Faculty or even graduate students often take pupils.
8. Professional performing orchestras such as symphonies, marching bands or concert bands often have members who give music instruction.
9. Music festivals, such as those put on by Kiwanis, will have contacts for private lessons.
10. Don't forget your local school. There will likely be a music teacher or someone in charge of the music program who can refer you to a private instructor.

HOW TO CHOOSE A TEACHER

Obviously, there are many ways you can locate a teacher, but once you do locate one, how are you going to decide which to choose? The first thing you have to determine is your purpose in having your child take music lessons. If it is primarily as a hobby or for the child's enjoyment, then qualifications may not be as important as personality and rapport. If you want your child to get a solid musical education and develop sound technique, then the musical training, methodology and experience of the teacher are more important. Let's look at some of these criteria.

Musical training Almost every music teacher trained in Canada will have passed exams offered by one of the musical organizations or societies listed at the end of this book. These organizations typically have a system of grades that measures performing achievement. This is usually followed by an advanced grade or diploma (ARCT is the best known). As well as practical instruction there are courses offered in music theory that are strongly recommended for anyone pursuing a career in teaching music. Some music teachers have taken music degrees at university. This does not guarantee a teacher will be better, but he or she will have a thorough grounding in more than one instrument.

Music teachers who are trained outside Canada will have different diplomas. One indicator of a well-trained teacher is voluntary membership in a registered music association. The membership requirements may vary from province to province, but they are consistently high.

Musical experience It is often said that there is no substitute for experience, but is that true for music? It is not necessary to be a virtuoso on a particular instrument to be a good teacher (just as a good hockey coach may not have been a good player). Most good teachers tend to be involved in performing in one form or another, as a church organist, community choir director or semi-professional musician. But a love of music will usually find some way to express itself.

A good music teacher will usually attend workshops and seminars, organize recitals for their colleagues or students or participate in music festivals and competitions. Often they will encourage similar involvement in their students, particularly in the form of competitions or recitals. Not every child will be the competitive type and a good teacher must be sensitive to each child, but it may be a good idea to be wary of a teacher who is unwilling to expose his students to *any* form of public performance.

Often teachers will take an extra step in recommending good concerts, shows or recordings to their students. The love of music is contagious and exposure to an enthusiastic and involved teacher can only enhance the learning opportunities for your child.

Rapport Though it may *seem* intangible, rapport is no less important than any of the other factors. In some cases, it may be the most important. If your child likes her teacher she is more likely to do what she is asked. If not, you can have a battle on your hands at practise time. The student's relationship with the teacher can affect her whole attitude toward learning music.

It is important to match your child's needs with the personality of the teacher. A teacher who demands excellence and a rigorous work ethic may not be the best choice for a beginner. One way to check out rapport would be to speak to a couple of the prospective teacher's students.

A final word of caution. Don't be swayed by price. Just because your child is just starting out doesn't mean he can get by with a less capable but more affordable teacher. In Japan, beginning Suzuki students are taught by the most experienced instructors. On the other hand, spending top dollar doesn't necessarily mean you will get the most appropriate instruction. Careful selection of the best teacher you can afford will in the long run make the learning experience more rewarding and result in more rapid progress.

ARRANGING LESSONS

Before you are ready to make a final choice of teacher, it is a good idea to arrange a meeting with the instructor, you and your child. If there is more than one choice of instructors, meet with each. You may have an opportunity to determine the rapport the teacher has with children. Once you have settled on a choice, it is time to set up the arrangements.

If you have decided on conservatory or music studio, all of the practical program details will be laid out. Private lessons tend to be a little less formal so you will need to find out:

1. How often the lessons are (usually weekly). Occasionally during preparation for recitals or exams, lessons may be a couple of times a week. Find out when holidays are to be taken by both you and the teacher. Often there is a summer hiatus that parallels the school year.
2. The length of lessons (typically a half-hour, but very young children may take 15 minutes and advanced students may take an hour).
3. Where the lessons take place (in your home, at a music school or in the instructor's studio). In most instances it is better to take the lessons at the music school or the teacher's studio where there are fewer distractions for the child and the teacher's resources are close at hand. Of course, very young children may not be ready to leave your home for a lesson.
4. Expectations for practise. Find out what the practise routine is and how much time should be spent between lessons.
5. How much involvement will be expected of you?
6. Payment method (some are pay-as-you-go, others are lump sum for a package of lessons).
7. What about missed lessons? Are they rescheduled? If not, do you get a refund if they were prepaid?
8. How much should they cost? This can vary as widely as the abilities of instructors. It will also depend on whether you are having a group or private lesson and the length of the les-

son. As with anything, market conditions and inflation will affect prices over time, but $15 to $20 per half-hour is quite common for private lessons. More advanced lessons of longer duration can be two or three times as much. Music academies will have different fee structures, depending on the programs offered. Typically they have a one-time enrolment fee followed by program fees that can be paid in instalments.

It is important to be clear about these details at the beginning because every music teacher will have a slightly different approach and set of expectations.

TALENT

The question of whether or not your child has any talent is bound to come up. The issue may occur very early, when your daughter walks up to the piano for the first time and plunks out a rudimentary melody she heard on television. Or it may happen well into the lesson program, when progress seems hopelessly stalled and frustration has set in for both you and your child.

Whether your child has talent depends to a great extent on what we mean by the term. When asked to define talent, some music teachers will flatly refuse to discuss it. It is a rather nebulous concept, as difficult to describe as love. Placido Domingo, the great operatic tenor, was once asked when it was that he discovered he had a talent for singing. He replied that he could always sing and that anyone can become a good singer, but his success as a singer could be attributed to 10 percent inspiration and 90 percent perspiration. What he was suggesting is that natural gifts alone are not enough to become successful. It is, however, possible to become successful with modest abilities along with determination and hard work.

Talent at a young age can be difficult to assess because children learn at varying rates. Some children pick new things up quickly but will soon hit a point where other kids will catch up. Early development can easily be confused with exceptional ability. Child prodigies like Mozart, who composed complex pieces of music before the age of six, are exceedingly rare. Nor does every musical prodigy become a successful performer.

RECITALS

Many music teachers like to arrange recitals for their pupils. A recital is a formal program consisting of pupils performing one or more of the pieces they have been working on. The audience consists of family and friends but recitals are usually open to the public. They can take place at a school or church or perhaps at the local library. Although a recital is not as structured or pressure-filled as a competition, it is an opportunity for your child to perform in public and demonstrate musical progress. A recital also serves as a goal to work toward during the year.

COMPETITIONS

If your child seems to have some musical aptitude and is enjoying the experience, his teacher is likely to suggest that he enter a competition. The teacher has two motivations. First, the child can benefit from the experience of performing in a competitive situation. Second, the reputation of the teacher is enhanced. (A teacher who has several students entered is probably a very competent teacher).

It is important to ensure that your child is both ready for a competition and emotionally able to handle the anxiety. Some children just do not handle the stress of being in front of people or the rigor of the practise required to prepare. You are the best judge of your child's emotional makeup. It is possible to turn a child off to music by pushing her into something she may not be ready for. Although some competitions will accept children as young as five, it is usually better to wait a couple of years until they are more mature.

The most common music competitions are those that make up the Kiwanis Festival. Sponsored by the Kiwanis clubs, they are held in every province in Canada, usually in the spring. The competition is usually a week long and is held in churches or other public buildings. Contestants can enter in a variety of categories including piano (solo and duet), violin, trumpet, clarinet, voice and choir. Age groups can range from under six to 18 years. In the older classes there are also "open" categories where eleven year olds, for instance, can compete against seventeen year olds.

Students prepare the pieces they play from their studies books. The pieces are divided up into categories of difficulty (A list, B list, etc.) and the student must choose a specified number of pieces from each list.

At the competition, entrants usually play from memory. They will be called up one by one according to their contestant number, and asked to play their selection for the adjudicator. After each piece, the adjudicator makes meticulous notes while everyone waits in nervous silence. After all the contestants have played, the adjudicator will address the competitors in turn, giving them comments about their performance. There will be plenty of positive comments, as well as suggestions for improvement. After each has been handed a mark, the ribbons are presented for first, second, third and participants.

It may be useful, if you are unsure about these events, to attend a Kiwanis Festival near you. Make sure you take in the particular age group your child is in *right now*. Knowing what to expect can eliminate a lot of the anxiety. Chances are your child will be encouraged to see that he can play "just like them".

CHAPTER SIX

School music

Music has always been a part of school curricula throughout Canada. Education is a matter of provincial jurisdiction, so each province will have slightly different expectations and guidelines for its music programming. In most cases the goals are fairly broad in scope; the means by which these are achieved will be left up to the individual schools and school boards.

The bad news, as mentioned earlier, is that the arts are under budget scrutiny and when cuts have to be made, music is often a target. Unless there is a change in philosophy, this trend is likely to continue and the integrity of music programming in schools cannot be counted on for the long term.

The good news is that, depending on the particular school board and the particular school, your child will get a basic understanding of musical concepts in elementary school. By junior high he should be able to take up an instrument and get some group lessons in performance.

MUSIC CURRICULUM

Most schools break down the grades into the following groupings:

```
Primary elementary  . . . . . . Kindergarten to grade 3
Junior elementary . . . . . . . . . . . . . . . Grade 4 to 6
Junior high or middle school  . . . . . . Grade 7 and 8
Senior high school  . . . . . . . . . . . . . Grade 9 to 12
```

In the primary grades, the focus is on developing listening and participation skills. Students will start out by learning to identify sounds, repetitive patterns, the difference between beat and rhythm in simple songs, and different speeds or tempos. From there they will learn some elementary musical terms and work on identifying the four families of orchestral instruments (strings, brass, woodwinds, percussion).

By the end of grade 3, kids should be able to apply the terms they learned earlier to actual music, although they will not learn to write them yet. Most school programming uses a combination of Orff and Kodály methodology and the emphasis is very much on singing. Some classes will use basic percussion instruments (blocks, sticks, triangles, xylophones, etc.) as well.

Who's teaching?

In most cases, music is taught by the regular classroom teacher, who may or may not have any formal musical training. They are, however, fully qualified school teachers. Some school boards have music teachers who go from class to class, or from school to school. Different provinces have different standards for qualifications to teach music so the standards can vary somewhat. It is important to remember that school music is geared toward providing that part of an overall education, and not toward creating musicians.

In the middle grades, the emphasis on learning the elements of music continues with singing and rhythm instruments. By grade 4, some classes may begin to learn the recorder. The names of the notes will be used along with the names of the pitches (A, B, C, D, etc.) By grade 6 students can often write music on the five-line staff. They may be able to distinguish between music from different periods and cultural backgrounds. Some will learn to identify basic structural concepts such as dynamics and key signatures.

While this all sounds very promising, elementary-school kids will rarely get a chance to actually touch a real orchestral or band instrument, let alone learn how to play one. Very few schools in the public or Catholic system have the funds to purchase these.

If you are hoping for an early start for your child, you will be disappointed. In most cases it is not until high school that there is an opportunity to actually take up an instrument. Even in those cases, instrumental instruction is just one of many options.

Junior high will continue the development of musical concepts. Occasionally there will be a band program or a strings program that parents can opt to have their kids take. These are increasingly few and far between and have limited availability due to class size. Students often share instruments because there are too few to go around.

One of the significant drawbacks to school music programs is that lessons are always in a group. Class sizes can be anywhere from 15 to 40, depending on the school. Individual instruction is out of the question. If a child requires extra help, or wants to go beyond the scope of the class, she will have a great deal of difficulty getting anything over and above normal classroom time.

HIGH SCHOOL

By the time your child reaches high school, the options for music expand considerably. Most high schools have band programs that can range from beginning to advanced level.

There are different types of band programs. **Stage bands** are like those you would see entertaining on television shows such as *Late Night with David Letterman*. They often have electric guitars and drums accompanying them and play mostly popular music and showtunes.

Concert bands are more like the traditional orchestral configurations we are used to in the symphony. There is much more focus on classical repertoire with some popular show music for variety. In many cases, there are no string sections but there is sometimes piano and electric guitar.

Marching bands are complete with drums, fifes and those enormous sousaphones that seem to dwarf their players. If your child is interested in a marching band, you need to be aware that there is usually a fancy uniform to be purchased and there will likely be some fundraising required. Marching bands also travel and enter competitions, sometimes involving overnight stays.

Wherever there are music programs, there is usually a **vocal program** of some sort. This may be actual voice classes or, more typically, a glee club or school choir. These are ideal for kids who like music but lack the means to pursue a musical instrument.

In addition to the band programs, there may be specific instrument programs, which can include any or all of the following: electric and acoustic guitar, piano, voice, strings, brass instruments, woodwinds and percussion. There is sometimes classroom instruction on music theory and history with a focus on classical music. Students may be encouraged to compose and perform their own music based on the principles learned.

Not all high schools offer all or any of these programs. In some cities, however, there are high schools that place a great deal of emphasis on the arts and may have extensive music programs. If this is a direction your child wants to take, you might want to look into the enrolment criteria for a school such as this.

UNIVERSITY AND BEYOND

Most universities offer degree programs in music. Additionally, there is often a master's program and in some larger universities, a doctoral program. Candidates for such programs are usually required to have achieved a certain grade level (usually grade 10) in one or more instruments. Being able to play the piano as well is a great asset.

There are also a number of prestigious programs that go beyond the normal university music programs such as the Eastman School of Music in Rochester, New York, the Juilliard School in New York City and the Glenn Gould School of Professional Music. These have very stringent entrance requirements so that only students with the greatest potential for excellence are admitted.

CHAPTER SEVEN

Choirs and church music

When considering musical opportunities for your child, don't forget about the instrument we are all born with - the voice. Choral music is perhaps the earliest musical form and among the most pleasing.

When we think of a choir we usually think of simply a group of people singing together. A choir, though, is a group with definite structure. The number of people can range from a handful to several hundred. Smaller groups of singers are often referred to as duos, trios and quartets for two, three and four voices respectively. As well, there are several types of choirs. They can be all female, all male, all children, all adults and a combination of the above.

One of the easiest places to look for an opportunity to make music is your place of worship. Many churches have a paid organist who doubles as a music director. Some larger congregations may have both positions. In addition to one or more adult choirs, there may be a children's choir.

If your church is lucky enough to have a children's choir, it will probably start off by learning unison pieces. Two- and three-part harmony may be attempted by older children at the discretion of the choir director. Children with little or no exposure to musical training will get some appreciation of melody, rhythm and pitch, but most of the effort is put into getting the sound right rather than understanding the background.

Many choir directors and church musicians are also qualified instructors. Often they will offer private lessons at the church or in the home. In some cases the church itself may sponsor group lessons for interested parishioners.

Another type of choir that can be a source of enjoyment for children is a bell choir. Some churches are fortunate enough to have a set of tuned hand bells, ranging in size from slightly smaller than a teacup to the size of a small pail. Each bell has a specified pitch that is stamped on the handle. Bell music is fairly easy to follow and each person is responsible for a certain number of bells, from one to as many as six or eight, depending on the complexity of the piece. Children can easily learn to handle the bells and all ages can participate equally in the music.

Although it is highly integrated into Christian worship, religious music is by no means limited to Christianity. Many other religions have well-developed musical expressions of their faith. In Judaism, for instance, the cantor leads the singing of the prayers and psalms at synagogue and holds a highly respected position in the temple.

COMMUNITY CHOIRS

Depending on the size of your community, there may be a number of amateur choirs for all ages. In almost all cases auditions will be required, especially if these are performing groups. The occasional exception to this may be a choir sponsored by a local service club who may have a come one, come all policy. The reason for the auditions is that the music being performed is generally more complex, involving three- and four-part harmony. This requires more advanced understanding of musical elements and the ability to read music.

The level of commitment is necessarily greater for choirs of this type. Typically rehearsals are every week, usually for a couple of hours, and sometimes a little longer before a major performance. The type of music performed is often more complex and demanding. It can range from traditional Christmas carols to cantatas such as Bach's *Wachet Auf*. Occasionally a more ambitious piece such as Bach's *St. Matthew Passion* will be performed. The concert season is usually concentrated around Christmas and Easter, with as many as 12 concerts occurring during Advent and Christmas.

Some choirs will schedule at least one out-of-town trip, which may require overnight accommodation. This may require some fundraising activities.

Fees for joining such choirs will vary, but you can expect around $200 per year for an average choir.

BARBERSHOP GROUPS

Also referred to as close harmony, barbershop music was popular at the beginning of the twentieth century. It was primarily sung by males in four-part harmony and gave rise to the phenomenon known as the barbershop quartet. It remains an enjoyable form of music today, and has the advantage of not requiring any instrumental accompaniment. There are amateur groups in many urban centers. The appeal of these groups tends to be mainly for an older crowd, but there are some children's groups as well. One of the largest groups is the Sweet Adelines, which enlists females only and has chapters throughout North America.

If your child is contemplating joining a performing choir, it is important to understand that he must have a real commitment to practices and rehearsals. It is not enough to simply learn the music and show up to perform. Rehearsals are critical for learning timing and cues from the conductor. Each piece of music has its idiosyncrasies and interpretations and these need to be learned by the group as a whole. Finally, choral music is a group experience and it is vital to sing shoulder to shoulder with your fellow singers to develop the blending of voices that makes a choir an instrument unto itself.

Another option to look into is **community theatre**. There are often musical productions put on for and by young people and they can provide wonderful musical experience. Again, auditions are probably required, but there are often smaller roles that are less demanding for kids.

CHAPTER EIGHT

Future careers in music

Once your child has a taste for music she may decide that she wants to make a living at it. As a parent you may have visions of the stereotypical starving artist eking out a meager existence and probably living at home. The old saying "Don't give up your day job" comes quickly to mind. But before you pass on this sage advice, you should know that there are a number of day jobs in music. It is very possible to earn a respectable living either performing music or working in a closely related field.

PERFORMING

While most aspiring musicians have the dream of becoming a star performer like their idols, the reality is that, like pro athletes, the number who make it is extremely small. There are, however, many other professional performing musicians. Some of these are full-time and some are part-time jobs. They all share one thing in common – these musicians are doing something they love.

Symphony musicians typically are university music graduates. They interview and audition for their positions. Symphony schedules are extensive and varied, requiring a great deal of rehearsal and practice. Symphony musicians often supplement their income by teaching music. In addition to performing with their orchestra, musicians will also perform with smaller groups such as chamber music ensembles. They will also go out into the community to schools to demonstrate and give presentations about their instruments and their music.

Classical music has a variety of other jobs within its own special niche:

- **Conductor** – responsible for choosing, interpreting and directing the music as well as the overall direction of the orchestra
- **Concertmaster/concertmistress** – usually leads rehearsals and is almost always the principal first violinist
- **Section leader** – sometimes called the principal player, who usually performs the solos or most complicated parts
- **Opera singer**
- **Managing director** – usually involved with the hiring of musicians and the day-to-day operations of the orchestra

Dance bands are groups that play at high-school or community dances. Almost all bands start out doing engagements such as these but it is grinding hard work for low pay. The hours are late, there is usually a great deal of travel and, after expenses are paid and the fee divided up among the band members, there is often barely enough to get the group to the next performance. Having said all this, it is possible for a dedicated and talented group to make a respectable living if they are prepared for the unstable lifestyle.

A performing musician will most likely have to join the local chapter of a musicians union. This will involve the payment of dues and the listing of your talent or specialty through the union booking organization. There is usually a fee scale set up for various types of acts or performances. While this may seem high-handed, it does have the effect of levelling the playing field. It is well known that performers trying to get started will perform for next to nothing just to get themselves known. The musicians union prevents performers from being taken advantage of by opportunistic club owners or booking agents.

There are other types of performing opportunities that, while not as glamorous as being a rock star, can be just as rewarding professionally and financially. These are **session musicians** – people who play the lush sounds of your favorite movie soundtrack or the music accompanying those snappy television commercials. Session musicians are usually relatively unknown to the public, but well paid if they are good. Some of these session musicians even go on to become stars in their own right, such as Barry Manilow who began by writing and playing commercial jingles for companies such as McDonald's. Session musicians enjoy a much more stable working environment, but their musical work can be just as demanding, often involving long and unusual hours.

Another type of session musician is the **background vocalist**. These are paid individuals who provide vocal support for the lead entertainer. They are often employed by music agencies or recording studios. Occasionally they can be freelance performers, doing this background work as a stepping stone to a bigger career.

Writing music is often viewed as a part-time career or hobby, but there are music publishing houses who employ full-time composers. Occasionally, some of those staff writers go on to fame as performers, such as Neil Sedaka, Carole King and Neil Diamond. The vast majority, however, toil away creating the music we hear on television, in the movies, in commercials and for many of the popular stars.

TEACHING

One of the obvious careers is that of a **school teacher** who specializes in music. A person must first become a fully qualified teacher. Certified teachers may upgrade their skills by taking music classes. Someone who has a degree in music must also enter teacher's college to obtain teacher certification.

Teaching private lessons also can provide a good source of income. Some musicians prefer the structured environment of a conservatory or music academy, which may provide a salary or commission. Others prefer the independence of offering private lessons as a self-employed teacher. In this case a person would be responsible for finding his own pupils and paying his own expenses.

Another potential career related to education is that of **music therapist**. This is gaining popularity as a method of treating children and adults with psychological problems such as autism.

CHURCH MUSIC

Many middle to large congregations have a **music** or **choir director** (occasionally referred to as minister of music.) This can be a significant position with a variety of responsibilities and is sometimes a full-time job. In addition to directing the choir, the music director may be involved in the selection of music for worship, hiring occasional additional musicians, performing or playing the organ and directing the organist or primary musician. (Often the music director is also the organist.)

The **cantor** is roughly equivalent to the music director in a Jewish synagogue or temple. The cantor leads the prayers and the singing of the psalms at worship. The cantor differs slightly in that he is a highly involved participant in the worship and must have a good voice to exercise leadership in singing. The cantor also can lead and direct choirs for worship.

The **church organist** is also a key position. In the absence of a music director, the organist is usually responsible for the musical life of the congregation. Depending on the size of the congregation, this can be either a full- or part-time position. Most church organists belong to an organization called the Royal Canadian College of Organists (RCCO), which sets standards for qualifications, sets fee guidelines and has a code of ethics. Most congregations try to follow the suggested fee structure.

POP MUSIC

A very popular form of musical entertainment for large group functions and dances, especially weddings, is the **disc jockey** or **deejay**. He provides the equipment and a vast library of musical selections catering to a variety of tastes. Some even provide karaoke, where the participants can sing along to instrumental accompaniment. A good deejay can earn several hundred dollars an engagement and can be kept quite busy. Beware, though – the work is mostly weekends!

MUSIC RETAIL

There are plenty of opportunities in the retail sector that, while not particularly high paying, offer close involvement in the business of music. **Music stores** that sell compact discs and cassettes need people who are knowledgeable about music in general. **Instrument retailers** require salespersons who know the instruments and are capable of doing demonstrations for prospective buyers. Often people involved in floor sales will also have an agreement with the store to supply lessons for clients on request, for an agreed fee over and above their salary. There are also potential jobs for **service and repair of musical instruments**. This could entail an apprenticeship period. Piano tuning is another potential career, sometimes coupled with piano instruction.

THE MUSIC BUSINESS

Music has a business side and there are jobs for people in organizing and scheduling events. Most performers have **personal managers** or **agents** who look after all the details of booking engagements, arranging for travel and accommodation and publicity. These people are usually paid a percentage of the performer's fee.

The other end of the business is the **booking agent**, who sometimes works for a talent firm or perhaps a specific venue. Such people will negotiate with the performer's agents, arranging for dates and arriving at a fee. On a larger scale there is the **concert promoter**, who is usually an entrepreneur. The concert promoter will negotiate with both agents and the local authorities to arrange a large concert. These can often be multiple engagements in several locations. A promoter is paid a percentage of the gate receipts.

Most large concert halls have a **business manager**. Although there is an increasing trend for these positions to be filled by business graduates, they are still often done by people with a music background.

Finally, all that sheet music comes from somewhere. **Music publishers** buy the right to publish from the writer in exchange for a royalty for each copy sold. Music publishers can be very large or very small. It is even possible for a performer to publish her own music.

Radio and Television Music has long been the lifeblood of radio. One of the most prominent jobs is the **disc jockey**. No matter what type of music you love, there is a radio station specializing in that format and it requires knowledgeable deejays in that music to present it to the listener. There is also the **program director**, who will often choose the music and control all on-air activity.

Television stations now produce all-music video programs and the **video jockey** is the personality who presents them to the viewer. Knowledge of the music is required, as well as the ability to conduct interviews with performers. Some television stations also have a music director who is responsible for all aspects of music programming.

Other opportunities include jobs in print media. Newspapers and magazines often have **music reporters** or **critics** who write articles, review performances and recordings and report on upcoming events. There are also freelance writers who specialize in writing articles and books specific to the music industry.

Recording The recording business is a multibillion-dollar industry with thousands of career opportunities. Many of these are filled by musicians and non-musicians alike. These can include:

- advertising sales
- director of publicity
- field merchandiser (someone who ensures enough of the product is properly displayed)
- record producer
- music arranger
- recording engineer (the person who handles the technical feat of putting all the sounds together)
- orchestrator (co-ordinates the musical performers in the studio)
- promotion and publicity personnel (we sometimes call them "hype artists")
- marketing manager and representatives
- copyist (transcribes the various musical parts for each performer)

CHAPTER NINE

Supporting your child in music

PRACTICE

Practice will without a doubt be the most challenging part of having a child involved in music lessons. Music practise is time not spent playing to an eight-year-old this can be intolerable. When it comes to a choice between piano practise and baseball or a computer game, be prepared for some parental "convincing".

Practise between lessons, however, is vital to learning. Many accomplished musicians will confide that they are grateful for the "encouragement" and support they received during their practice time.

Getting started seems to be the point of struggle for both parents and kids. One of the best ways to cope with this is to establish a familiar, easy-to-follow routine. If you watch a baseball player, for instance, he will go through the same warm-up routine before each game. This is to help him focus. Focus is also applicable to music practice. Your child's teacher will probably have suggestions, but a typical routine might consist of:

- *warm-up* – perhaps a favorite song or scales. Getting the fingers, lips or voice limbered up will help before tackling the difficult parts.
- *drills* – Perhaps a new song is being learned, or a specific exercise has been assigned by the teacher. Trouble spots should be given extra attention.
- *wrap-up* – Your child may have a song he or she is good at and enjoys playing. It is good to end in a positive mood.

Picking the right time is important. Here are a few situations to avoid:

- Right after school. Your child has just put in a full day and is likely to need time to unwind, just as most of us do from our jobs.
- Before bedtime. Although this depends to some degree on the child, kids need to be able to concentrate to practise effectively and are usually not at their best when they are tired.
- Early in the morning. Some kids are "morning people" and this may work for them. However, mornings are often chaotic times and you may not want to start your day listening to trumpet practice.
- During favorite TV programs. You don't want to deal with resentment. (If there are too many favorites, that may be a separate issue.) Also, if the neighborhood kids are just about to start up a weekly ball game, that may not be a good time either.
- Before mealtime or snacktime. It is difficult to concentrate on an empty stomach.

Although a regular practice time is important, there may be some negotiation and flexibility required. An important event or family activity may have to take precedence, but the two of you can work out an alternate time.

Although it can be frustrating when you have to nag your child to practise, *don't* resort to threats: "We spend a fortune on music lessons for you and if you don't practise, we may as well cancel them." This may run through your mind, but if you stop and think you would never dream of saying, "If you don't do your homework, we'll stop sending you to school." Encouragement will go a lot further than threats.

Practice times will vary according to the student and the teacher. Beginning students often have 15 minute practices. Twenty minutes to half an hour is typical for intermediate pupils. Advanced students will usually spend 45 minutes to an hour. Practice does not need to be long to be effective. Too long a time can lead to daydreaming and resentment.

HOW YOU CAN HELP

First and foremost, it is important to be as accepting as possible of your child's efforts. This can be particularly challenging for a student in the Suzuki violin program. You are likely to be subjected to a pretty horrendous racket, but your child does not need to know this. The parents' attitude toward practice will often be reflected in the child's attitude. For instance, making your child practise the clarinet in the basement to cut down on the noise sends the message that your child's music lessons are an inconvenience. You may have to rearrange your schedule to accommodate music lessons. This indicates you place a priority on the lessons.

Many instruments can be practised at low volumes. This is helpful when practice must be done while others are around. Electric keyboards have volume controls and electric guitars can be played without the amplifier turned on. Brass instruments sometimes have a device called a mute that softens the sound when placed in the end of the horn. Even the drums can be practised relatively quietly with a set of practice pads, purchased at a music store.

You may wonder just how much you should be involved in your child's practice. This varies from child to child and from program to program. Younger children may need the presence of an adult. This may mean sitting beside the child to offer encouragement, or simply sitting across the room reading a book or newspaper. Parents of children in a Suzuki violin program may be encouraged to play along with their children. By the age of nine or 10, many children are capable of practising independently, though some may require monitoring. If you do not want to be, or cannot be, present during practice, make sure the teacher writes down carefully the steps and goals so that the child can keep focused. One important thing to remember is that, just as in your child's regular schooling, as long as he is involved, you will be too.

You can support your child by providing a good environment to practise in. Some of these may seem obvious, yet can be taken for granted:

- Ensure that there is adequate light. This may involve a special piano light, for instance.
- Provide a space that has some privacy and is free from distractions. This could require other family members to co-operate by staying clear. If your child plays the drums, this should not be a problem.
- Provide a music stand.
- Make sure the instrument is stored in a safe and convenient place. Making it difficult to get at can be used as an excuse not to practise.
- If the music teacher approves, provide a metronome.

A metronome is an adjustable device that ticks off a steady beat and aids the musician in keeping a correct and consistent tempo. There are two main types of metronomes: a basic mechanical one that winds up and electronic models that have a whole host of features. Prices can range from $30 for a basic model to over $100 for the fancy ones.

DEALING WITH FRUSTRATION

Inevitably, there will come a time when practice becomes a problem. This can be for legitimate reasons or just plain old frustration. Legitimate reasons for not practising can include:

- sickness or injury
- family commitments or vacations
- heavy regular schoolwork, such as exams or term papers
- important social functions such as birthdays, graduations or bar mitzvahs

Frustration can be the most difficult thing to deal with as a parent, because we are not only dealing with the child's frustration, but our own as well.

The key to handling these situations is to find out the cause. Children like to make progress and are often used to learning quickly. In studying an instrument, there will inevitably be **plateaus** where little or no progress is evident. This is normal. One of the most common times for a plateau to occur is around February. Most school teachers agree that Christmas is long past, Easter is a long way off and the winter blahs affect just about everybody. Focus on the fun of playing and encourage your child to play favorite pieces. Some music teachers recognize this and will schedule a March recital to work toward.

Here are a few things you can say when your child doesn't want to practise:

1. It's the only way you are going to get better.
2. It makes us proud to hear you play.
3. Playing in a band/orchestra/group is fun.
4. You'll never find out how good you are.
5. If I don't insist on your practising now, you'll complain to me later when it gets difficult.

If your child is feeling frustrated because she is not achieving results from her practice, perhaps it is time to sit down with the music teacher and discuss changes to the practice routine, or even a different approach or method of teaching.

Sticking to practice schedules can be a chronic problem for some students. Some teachers recommend a contract for a child to sign, in which they promise to practise a certain amount each day. Below is an example of such a contract.

Practice Contract

This contract is a promise by the pupil to the teacher and parent to practise a certain length of time each day, for a certain number of days each week.

I, _____, student of _____, promise to practise for _____ minutes or more each day for a minimum of _____ days each week. If I miss one or more days of regular practice, I will make it up the next day or on the weekend. I also promise to complete any assigned homework.

Student's signature _____
                    Date _____

Parent's signature _____
                    Date _____

Instructor's signature _____
                    Date _____

Another useful way of encouraging discipline in practice is to keep a weekly log. There can be a certain satisfaction in seeing those little spaces filled up as the days go by. Practise records can be obtained at most music stores, or you can draft your own version similar to the one below.

Weekly Practice Schedule

Name _____

Week of _____

Assignments	Mon.	Tue.	Wed.	Thu.	Fri.	Sat.	Sun.	Weekly total
Total time								

Parent's signature _____

Date _____

Comments from parent to teacher

Comments from teacher to parent

MOTIVATION

Ideally the best motivation is the sheer love of making music. Most kids will experience this, but let's face it, routine will kick in and it will be hard to keep going. We all need a little motivation from time to time. The key is knowing what to do and when to do it.

Praise is one of the most powerful motivators going. It is critical that you pay attention to your child's progress. Catch him doing something well and tell him how much you like it. Younger children are especially eager to show you and the rest of the family what they can do.

Speaking of rewards, is it appropriate to bribe your child? This is something you can discuss with your child's instructor. Younger children will often respond well to a judiciously dispensed treat, whether its stickers or candy. Make sure you and the teacher are of one mind on the nature of the treat.

A brief little concert for visiting relatives or friends can be a positive reinforcement. Children usually love to show their stuff. Recitals with other students can be set up with your instructor. These can be fun and give the students a goal to work toward.

There are also numerous games, flash cards and computer programs (available at most music stores) that can inject fun into your child's music education.

Just as praise is a powerful motivator, the threat of punishment can be a deterrent. Nagging or threatening can lead to a negative association with practice. Avoid punishment for not completing practice. Making your child do the dishes for a month will get you lots of clean dishes but is not likely to improve the practice environment. Instead, try positive reinforcements such as rewards or a practice log.

In spite of all these little suggestions, nothing succeeds like success. The better your child plays, the more he will enjoy practising. In the beginning especially, practice is fun and parents should take advantage of this so that the child gets better sooner, and success fuels their enthusiasm.

WHEN YOUR CHILD WANTS TO QUIT

Sometimes the inevitable recessions will develop into complete frustration, resulting in statements like "I hate this, I don't want to do it anymore", or "I don't want to play the piano, I want to play the trumpet". This is where you, the parent, must take stock of the situation. You will need to determine if your child has hit a plateau, is going through a phase or really wants to quit. If she really wants to quit, you must find out the reason.

Study of a musical instrument is a long process, often lasting a lifetime. It is, therefore, a good idea to at least give a commitment of one year to an instrument and teacher before re-evaluating the situation. Sometimes, though, a change of instrument or teacher may be called for.

In determining if the instrument is the problem, it is wise to re-examine how it was chosen. For example, your daughter may have wanted to take up piano because her best friend had done so. At first, lessons go well, but after a while her friend progresses much faster, and soon your daughter is frustrated at not being able to keep up. You are sure she likes to make music, yet this may be a situation where a switch of instruments is appropriate. Once the pressure to keep up with her peers is removed, she can progress at her own pace.

Personality also plays a part. An outgoing child who likes to be with others may find that solitary violin lessons do not suit him. Perhaps a band instrument, such as the trumpet or clarinet, will result in a more enjoyable learning experience. These instruments often involve concert bands, stage bands and marching bands, which may be better suited to a more social personality. The reverse can also be true: the child's personality may be better suited to an instrument such as the guitar, which can be self-taught to some degree and is conducive to fooling around on when the spirit moves him. You are the best judge of your child's personality, and it would be wise to take this into account when helping him select a suitable instrument.

There may be another reason some kids want to quit: the teacher. Some instructors, while being very nice people and fine musicians, may not have the right temperament or attributes to be an effective teacher. You as a parent need to be aware of the teacher's methods and performance. Listen to your child's comments to get clues about any potential problems. It may be a good idea to attend a lesson periodically, just to get an idea of what's going on.

Here are a few signs that may indicate it is appropriate to consider a new teacher:

- lack of homework instructions or practice assignments
- overly negative comments
- inattentiveness during lesson times (telephone conversations or family and friends interrupting the lesson)
- indifference to your child's lack of progress

If you decide to make a change, it is best to remember that children, especially younger ones, develop attachments to teachers and you will want to do so in a way that is least upsetting to the child. A smooth transition is preferable. If you decide in the spring that things aren't working out, then as long as the situation isn't destructive, try to wait until the summer break before making the change.

Sit down with your child and discuss the change honestly. You may tell your child that you aren't happy with the way the lessons are going and you are making a change to someone who will make them more interesting and exciting. You may also suggest that she is getting older and is ready for a more challenging instructor. It is all right to admit that you made a mistake in choosing a teacher the first time. We all make mistakes. Whatever approach you take, try to put a positive spin on it so your child will continue to have enthusiasm for music.

One of the most important ways you can support your child's musical education is to incorporate music into your leisure activities. Simply shelling out money for books and lessons and driving her back and forth won't necessarily build an appreciation and enthusiasm for music. We need to expose our children as much as we can to music and emphasize the enjoyment it brings.

MUSIC IN THE HOME

Having the radio on softly in the background can have a soothing effect on children as well as adults. If you pay attention, you'll hear humming and tapping in time to the music and even the occasional "ta-ti-ti-ta" you may have heard during lesson times. Having music in the background (judiciously chosen) while doing homework can stimulate your child's creative juices. Pay attention to the music your child likes and make a gift of a CD by her favorite artist. Choose some music together. You may be surprised to find some common interest.

The local library carries a number of children's recordings ranging from preschool to preteen. The adult sections will have classical, jazz, blues, pop and showtunes.

Don't forget books about music. If, for instance, your child is learning the guitar, there are several fine books on the history of the guitar, with loads of pictures. Often manufacturers of instruments such as the guitar, violin or piano publish a retrospective of their business with features on many of the finest players. Autobiographies of many famous musicians, especially in popular music, are favorites of young readers.

CONCERTS

Try to take in as much live music as you can. Watching an accomplished musician play the same instrument as your child is learning can be a good learning experience as well as a source of inspiration. If your community has a symphony orchestra, take your child to a concert. There are often programs of lighter selections geared to families. For some, the cost of symphony tickets may be out of reach, but there are often shorter free concerts put on by smaller ensembles purely for the fun of performing. Watch your local newspaper. If you get a chance, you may be able to have your child meet the musician after the performance. This can leave a lasting impression on children and serve as a great motivator. Some of the places you may find free or low-cost concerts are:

- museums
- libraries
- places of worship
- high schools
- local universities and colleges
- parades
- sporting events (skip the hot-dog stand and watch the half-time show!)

Summertime is a great time for free stuff. There are often free concerts in parks and, if the weather is nice, you can take along a picnic lunch and make a fine day of it. The key here is variety. Good music comes in all forms.

CHAPTER TEN

The language of music

WHAT IS MUSIC?

One definition of music could be simply "organized sound". It's not quite as simple as that, though. Random sounds are sometimes incorporated into compositions to convey a particular idea or feeling. There are, however, certain conventions and principles that are followed by all musicians.

As we mentioned before, music is like a language. It has its own set of symbols, rules for writing and reading these symbols and a host of terms to convey the properties of sound to the person reading the music. In order to better understand what's involved in teaching and learning a musical instrument, let's take a basic look at how some of these ideas fit together.

Musical sound (as opposed to noise) is made up of tones. Each tone has four key properties: **pitch**, **duration**, **intensity** and **timbre**.

Pitch

The relative highness or lowness of a tone is referred to as pitch. (In science this is called frequency.) Pitch is measured by the number of vibrations per second. More vibrations per second means a higher pitch and fewer vibrations, a lower pitch. The distance between two pitches is called an interval. In music, pitches are named using the first seven letters of the alphabet, A through G, repeated over and over again. The piano keyboard provides a useful diagram since its 88 keys represent almost all of the pitches used in Western music.

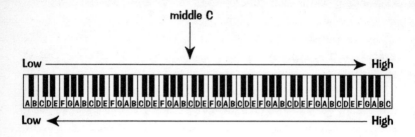

The white keys show the pitches and their names. Note the repeating pattern of the letters. The interval between pitches of the same letter is called an octave. The pitches are divided *within* an octave in one of two ways. Notice that there are seven white keys before a letter repeats. This seven-step octave is called a diatonic scale. If you count the black *and* the white keys, there are twelve steps or intervals. This is called a chromatic scale. Each step in this 12-pitch octave is called a semitone.

Duration

If you think of sheet music as a kind of map, then music has its own system of co-ordinates like the grid squares on a map. The five lines that make up the staff and the notes or symbols we put on the lines are our musical map.

The grand staff

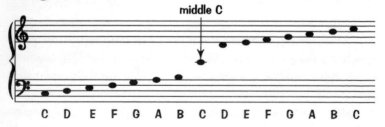

The lines and the spaces between them are given names corresponding to the first seven letters of the alphabet, A through G. Each set of five lines and four spaces is called a **staff**. Most music consists of at least two sets of these five lines. This is called the **grand staff**. A symbol is placed at the beginning of each staff to show the exact pitch represented by each line and space. The one on top is called the **treble clef** and, in piano music, these notes are usually played by the right hand. The lower set of lines called the **bass clef**, are lower-sounding and are played with the left hand. In vocal music, the soprano and alto lines, usually sung by women, are on the treble clef, while the tenor and bass usually sung by men are on the lower or bass clef.

There are other clefs that are sometimes used by other instruments. The cello, for instance, uses a **tenor clef**. Reading music from these other clefs can be a struggle for beginning students and is usually reserved for advanced players.

One way children are taught to remember the names of the notes for the lines and spaces on the staff is with the use of a mnemonic device. The lines in the treble clef are from top to bottom E, G, B, D and F or Every Good Boy Does Fine. The spaces are F, A, C and E which spell the word FACE. The lines in the bass clef are G, B, D, F and A or Good Boys Do Fine Always and the spaces are A, C, E and G.

The space in between the two sets of lines represents pitches as well. There are three pitches between the staffs, B, C and D. The C falls directly in the middle and for this reason is called *middle C*.

That curly thing that looks like an upper case S in handwriting actually represents the letter G. This symbol indicates that the second line from the bottom is the G above middle C and it is called the treble or G clef. In the lower staff the symbol that looks like a curve with two dots in front of it represents the letter F and signifies that the fourth line from the bottom is the F below middle C.

Occasionally, you will see pitches written above or below the staff. In this case short lines called ledger lines are used so performers don't lose track of where they are.

Let's return to the piano keyboard for a moment. We learned that the white keys are given the names A through G, but what about the black keys? Each one of those black keys actually has two names. The black key between middle C and D is called C sharp or D flat. The symbol for a sharp note is "#" and a flat note looks much like a lower case "b".

Duration

The notes indicate how long a particular pitch is to be played or sung. The rests tell us how long a performer goes without making a sound.

	Notes	Rests
whole	𝅝	▬
half	𝅗𝅥	▬
quarter	𝅘𝅥	𝄽
eighth	𝅘𝅥𝅮	𝄾
sixteenth	𝅘𝅥𝅯	𝄿
thirty-second	𝅘𝅥𝅰	𝅀

The lines of the staff are divided into sections called **bars** or **measures**. At the beginning of a piece of music there are a couple of numbers that usually look like a fraction. This is the **time signature** and it tells us how many beats are in each measure and the basic note value of a single beat. For instance, the time signature of 3/4 means that there are three beats per measure and a quarter note counts as one beat. If the time signature is 6/8, then there are six beats per measure and an eighth note counts as one beat.

Another important part of rhythm is tempo, or how fast the music is played. You are likely to see a lot of Italian words like *adagio*, *largo* and *allegro*. Most music also lists a numeral that indicates the number of beats per minute, e.g., 100-112. You can set a metronome to this number and follow the ticks to keep the tempo. Here is a list of the most common tempos:

largo - very slow
adagio - somewhat slow
allegro - fast
presto - very fast
prestissimo - just about as fast as you can
ritardando - slow down at the end

lento - slow
andante - moderate
vivace - lively

If you look at a piece of music, you will see the notes written in two ways. In some cases they follow one another in a horizontal pattern. These notes are played consecutively. Others are written vertically, that is, one on top of the other. There may be two or three or as many as five. These notes are played simultaneously. This is often referred to as a chord.

Dynamics

There are also cues in a piece of music that tell you how loud or soft to play. These characteristics are usually referred to as dynamics. Once again there is a barrage of Italian terms for dynamics, but thankfully they are represented by letters. P stands for *piano*, which means soft, and F stands for *forte*, which means loud. If the letters are doubled, it means very soft or very loud. If there is an M before the F it means midway between soft and loud.

Sometimes the music requires a building or decreasing of volume. This is symbolized by the use of an elongated < or > sign.

Here are the most common words for dynamics:

crescendo	– getting louder
decrescendo	– getting softer
piano	– softly
pianissimo	– very soft
forte	– loud
fortissimo	– very loud
mezzo forte	– medium loud
mezzo piano	– moderately soft

Timbre

The last quality of tone is timbre. This describes the characteristics that distinguish the sound of one instrument from another. Timbre is determined by a variety of factors, including the size of the instrument, the shape and the material it is made from. Understanding how this works is more the job of a physics student. The musician needs only to know that changing these factors changes the timbre.

CHAPTER ELEVEN

Appreciating music

There is no such thing as a non-musical person. There are some families whose interests, for one reason or another, do not include music. However, if you ask such people, they know what they like and don't like to listen to. Even if both parents ignore music, a child will be exposed to it through radio, television and school. Children are naturally attracted to music and musical things. If you pay attention to the most popular children's television programs, they will usually have a high musical content.

Whether we consider music an important part of our lives or not, we can still provide exposure to and enjoyment of music for our children.

The music of the Western world is categorized in two ways: classical music, sometimes called "art" or "serious music", and popular music, which includes folk, jazz, country, blues, rock 'n' roll, etc.

CLASSICAL TO MODERN

Though classical music sounds "high brow", many of its themes and forms are still popular today. Bugs Bunny humiliated Elmer Fudd to Rossini's *Barber of Seville* overture. Many other Warner Brothers' cartoons made liberal use of popular classical melodies that your children would recognize instantly. Walt Disney made the full-length feature *Fantasia* based on music by Tchaikovsky, Beethoven, Stravinsky and others, that has timeless appeal.

What we call classical music today was considered the popular music of its time. We can trace music as far back as 30,000 years as a result of archaeological discoveries of rudimentary instruments.

The Bible mentions flutes and harps, which were often used by shepherds to soothe restless flocks and pass idle hours.

Western music really began to develop, though, in the Middle Ages. Music was used extensively in worship and took the form of plainsong, or what we refer to today as Gregorian chant. It consists of a single melodic line sung unaccompanied, either alone or in unison. Recently, Gregorian chant has acquired a new following as a relaxing background music. For active listening, most children would not be attracted to it, but played softly it may serve as a good relaxer for nap or bedtime.

Outside the church, music was written for the royal court, or was provided by wandering minstrels and troubadours. Again, the melody line was simple. Often sung by one person and sometimes accompanied by a flute or other medieval instruments such as the lute.

By the mid fifteenth century, music began to develop what we call a polyphony, or counterpoint. Instead of a single melody, two or more melodies were superimposed to add a texture to the music. The Renaissance, from about 1450 to 1600, was dominated by church music. Secular music consisted of court music, particularly dances. Instruments began to be played on their own not simply to accompany vocals and music was written specifically for lute, organ and harpsichord. Some of this is delightful music, but of very limited appeal to kids. Most Renaissance music is, at best, stately. Some Renaissance composers to sample are Palestrina, Thomas Tallis, John Dunstable and Josquin Des Pres.

The 1600s saw the beginning of the **Baroque period**, which lasted until about 1750. This was the time of Newton, Rembrandt, Jonathan Swift, Samuel Johnson and John Milton. Science and the arts were in full flower, so it's no surprise that music underwent tremendous development as well. Vocal music flourished with the creation of operas, oratorios and cantatas. Other instrumental genres, such as the concerto and sonata, took shape. Italy, in particular, became a great contributor to musical development and Italian became the language of music. Even operas by German and French composers were written in Italian.

The Baroque period gave us some of the names we find familiar today: Handel, Bach, Vivaldi and Telemann are just a few.

The **Classical period** is generally regarded as 1750 (which is when Bach died) to about 1825 (Beethoven died in 1827). The early 1700s saw the invention of the piano, which quickly supplanted the harpsichord as the keyboard instrument of choice.

The sonata (for one or two instruments) and concerto (for solo instrument and orchestral accompaniment) became popular genres. The four-movement symphony became an important musical form and Joseph Haydn, who remarkably composed over 100 of them, came to be regarded as the father of the classical symphony. Opera continued to grow in popularity, especially after the contributions of Mozart, who dared to compose opera with German librettos (texts) instead of the traditional Italian. Another important form that developed was the string quartet (usually two violins, a viola and a cello). There are some particularly masterful works for this genre by all the major composers.

Classical period music is characterized by its great emotion. Complex harmonies and larger orchestras lead to a bigger, more dramatic and expressive sound. Individual parts were written for most instruments, further adding to the texture. Loud and soft passages helped to heighten the drama and emotion, especially in the later work of Beethoven.

This period gave us many of the composers who are regarded with great reverence today. Mozart, Beethoven, Schubert and Haydn all produced work which, taken on their own, could define a musical period.

The **Romantic period** (1825-1910) is characterized by individual expression, emotionalism and sometimes a dreamlike quality. The Romantic composers wore their hearts on their sleeves. They used for their subjects romantic novels and poems. Nationalistic music supplied themes and local folk melodies found their way into many compositions. Long, expressive melodies, with colorful harmony and instrumentation, were hallmarks of this period, with composers such as Brahms, Mendelssohn, Tchaikovsky, Wagner, Verdi and Chopin. Orchestration was supreme, with some orchestras exceeding 100 musicians. Most of the instruments kids play today took their form at this time.

The **Modern era** (1910-present) continued the fast pace of musical development of the Romantic period. Harmonies have become increasingly complex and the level of experimentation has grown exponentially. Modern composers have made extensive use of a technique called dissonance; some have made use of atonal or 12-tone scales to develop this new kind of sound. Emphasis is often on creating "sound pictures". This period took its inspiration from the impressionist movement in the visual arts during the late nineteenth century and composers such as Claude Debussy are often referred to as impressionist composers. The tone poem, developed by Franz Liszt and Richard Strauss, became an important musical form in the early twentieth century.

Up until the twentieth century, North America was not a player in musical history or development. Both Antonin Dvorák and Paul Hindemith spent time in America and were influenced by American folk melodies. Later in the twentieth century George Gershwin, Aaron Copland and Leonard Bernstein produced some fine music that will certainly endure.

Although Canadian composers are little known, there are several performers and conductors who have achieved considerable international acclaim. These include: Glenn Gould, Jon Vickers, Maureen Forrester, Mario Bernardi, Ben Heppner, Teresa Stratas, Charles Dutoit. Recordings by these Canadian stars are readily available.

DISCOGRAPHY

A selection of recommended listening for each period is listed below. The pieces are meant to be representative of the composers work as well as having some appeal to children. Check out the local library to sample them.

Renaissance

There's not much here that is readily available and it is of limited appeal to children. The most noteworthy person of the era is:

Palestrina *Missa Papae Marcelli*

Baroque

Johann Sebastian Bach	*Brandenburg Concerto No. 2*
	Toccata and Fugue in D minor
George Frideric Handel	*Messiah*
	Royal Fireworks Music
Antonio Vivaldi	*The Four Seasons*
Johann Pachelbel	*Canon in D major*

Classical

Wolfgang Amadeus Mozart	*Eine Kleine Nachtmusik*
	Symphony No. 40 in G minor
	Divertimento in F
Ludwig van Beethoven	*Piano Sonata No. 14 in C-sharp minor (Moonlight)*
	Symphony No. 5 in C minor
Franz Schubert	*Symphony No. 8 (Unfinished)*
	Piano Quintet in A (Trout)
Joseph Haydn	*Symphony No. 94 in G (Surprise)*
	Symphony No. 101 in D (Clock)

Romantic

Johannes Brahms	*Symphony No. 1*
	Hungarian Dances
	Violin Concerto in D
Peter Ilich Tchaikovsky	*Ballet Music (Nutcracker, Sleeping Beauty)*
	1812 Overture
	Romeo and Juliet
Franz Liszt	*Hungarian Rhapsody No. 2*
Felix Mendelssohn	*Hebrides Overture (Fingals Cave)*
	A Midsummer Night's Dream
Edvard Grieg	*Peer Gynt Suite*
Johann Strauss	*Waltzes*

Modern

Maurice Ravel	*Bolero*
Sergey Prokofiev	*Peter and the Wolf*
George Gershwin	*Rhapsody in Blue*
Leonard Bernstein	*West Side Story*

POPULAR MUSIC

Popular music's roots come out of the secular music of the sixteenth and seventeenth centuries. Court music was meant for the stately dances of dukes and duchesses, but the common folk took the melodies and applied their own words and rhythms.

Operetta is even more accessible than opera. It falls into the category of light classic and is a blend of opera and theatre. Dialogue is spoken instead of sung and serves to connect several lavish song and dance numbers. Plots are often farcical and usually serve to send up the aristocracy or establishment. You could say they were the precursor to the Broadway musical, and they still enjoy considerable popularity today. The pre-eminent creators of operetta were Gilbert and Sullivan who wrote 13 operettas dating from the late nineteenth century, most of which are still widely performed. Humor was a feature of most operettas and patrons often left the theatre humming or singing one of the melodies. Gilbert and Sullivan operettas are frequently presented in high-school music or theatre programs.

Speculation has it that many popular nursery rhymes began this way. *Mary, Mary, Quite Contrary* is reputedly about Mary Queen of Scots and her four maids in waiting (also named Mary). *Hey Diddle Diddle* is said to have been a humorous description of Queen Elizabeth I who was fond of dancing. Even more interesting is the story of *Little Jack Horner* who was a messenger carrying a pie to Henry VIII into which had been baked the deeds to several wealthy pieces of land. The enterprising messenger named Jack Horner opened the pie and swiped one of the prime deeds for himself a plum indeed.

Country music has become quite sophisticated and so diversified that it is difficult to define. The beginnings of what would become country music are firmly rooted in rural America, and in particular the South. Deeply influenced by gospel and blues, country music deals with the issues faced by ordinary people – love and loss. Styles range from mournful hurtin' music to joyful tunes to get you dancing. Children are often drawn to the happy sing-along tunes that were early country staples. Songs such as *Turkey in the Straw*, *Red River Valley*, *Home on the Range*, and even *Rudolph the Red-nosed Reindeer* were all country hits.

Blues is predominantly an adult genre but it's worthy of mention because of its significant influence on the three most commercial forms of popular music: jazz, rock and country. It emerged around the end of the slave era of the southern United States. Itinerant singers (usually male) accompanied themselves with guitar or harmonica and sang about love, freedom, sex and the sorrows of life. The advent of the electric guitar and the addition of drums provided an urban flavor, which found its way into what would become rock 'n' roll.

Jazz is music that emphasizes improvisation. Some of us would probably think of early jazz/ragtime as saloon music. The image of a solitary piano player jangling along to a somewhat raucous crowd comes readily to mind. Those early entertainers had to think and play quickly, reacting to the mood of the clientele. Often they had to make things up on the spot, and this is probably where improvisation began.

> **Ragtime music** is familiar to many of us in the style of Scott Joplin's *The Entertainer*, featured in the academy award-winning movie *The Sting*, and other classic songs such as *Maple Leaf Rag* and *Tiger Rag*. While the names may not be familiar, the melodies will be instantly recognizable to most.

Dixieland jazz came from New Orleans as traditional southern hymns sung and played in funeral processions. On the way back from the cemetery, the musicians would break into up-tempo versions of these hymns or ragtime tunes. The music became popular in clubs and soon found its way into urban centers such as Chicago and New York, where it acquired a character all its own. Names such as Louis Armstrong, King Oliver and Pete Fountain are still much admired.

In the 1930s jazz developed a new form called swing. Its emphasis on big band arrangements and dance rhythms made swing popular throughout North America and Europe. Swing music seems to appeal to kids, probably because it is first and foremost dance music. Glenn Miller, Benny Goodman and Tommy Dorsey were some of the best and most popular bandleaders.

After World War II, jazz returned to a style featuring small combos and solo instrumentals again with great emphasis on improvisation. Some of the famous names of the era include Charlie Parker, Thelonius Monk and Dizzy Gillespie, whose bulging cheeks and deformed trumpet became a jazz icon. The big-band sound did not totally disappear, as Duke Ellington, Count Basie and Buddy Rich continued to produce fine recordings into the 1970s. Jazz continued to evolve under the influence of the beat generation with artists such as Miles Davis, John Coltrane and Thelonius Monk achieving enormous popularity among jazz aficionados. Today, the Spitfire Band and Rob McConnell and the Boss Brass are a couple of Canadian examples who continue to popularize big-band music.

Rock 'n' roll is the most recent form of popular music. It was born in the 1950s out of rhythm and blues, which was popular among black audiences. Rhythm and blues in turn borrowed elements of blues, gospel and jazz. As young people began to buy records, the music changed to reflect the interests of this new audience. Lyrics were written around teen and adolescent themes. The music was geared toward dance rhythms and the rock 'n' roll phenomenon was born.

> The term "rock 'n' roll" was first used to describe this new music by a Cleveland disc jockey named Alan Freed. He disliked the term "race music" that was being used to describe rhythm and blues at the time. He used it for the first time on his radio program in 1951, and the youth of the day, eager to find their own musical niche, adopted it as their own.

The first superstar of rock 'n' roll was Elvis Presley, who burst onto the music scene in 1955. With a style that combined blues with a fast country and western beat, and a dynamic stage presence complete with gyrating hips and gestures, he caused a sensation among teenagers of the time. Several other performers followed in the same vein, such as Chuck Berry, Roy Orbison, The Everley Brothers and many others. All wrote songs based on teen angst and rollicking good times, with teens and young adults buying records by the millions.

> Rock music is a varied and complex genre, almost impossible to define. There have been many styles that have come and gone; all have a unique sound. Among these are: surf music, acid rock, folk rock, heavy metal, bubble gum, motown, disco, punk rock, rap, reggae, grunge. The only rule is there are no rules, and it is vital that you as a parent be fully aware of the content. Some of this music has lyrics that are openly sexual or violent.

Suggested listening for rock 'n' roll

During the early years of rock 'n' roll right up until the 1980s, the main formats for listening were the vinyl record and the cassette. Most of the recordings made today are on compact disc. The vinyl record has receded into the world of collectibles. As a result, it may be difficult to find original works by some of the "classic" rock 'n' roll artists. There are several good compilations available on compact disc or cassette that can give you a good example of the music of each artist.

Below is a list of several performers who represent the development of rock 'n' roll. They are listed approximately in order of appearance, along with a representative song by each. It must be stressed that this list is not a "best of" list, but just a sampling. These are suggested for their appeal to kids as well as adults.

Elvis Presley	*Jailhouse Rock*
Chuck Berry	*Johnny B. Goode*
Little Richard	*Tutti Frutti*
The Everley Brothers	*Bye Bye Love*
Chubby Checker	*The Twist*
The Beatles	*She Loves You*
The Beach Boys	*Surfin U.S.A.*
The Monkees	*Last Train to Clarksville*
The Archies	*Sugar Sugar*
Three Dog Night	*Joy to the World*
Elton John	*Crocodile Rock*
Bee Gees	*Stayin' Alive*
Queen	*We Are the Champions*
Michael Jackson	*Beat It*
Technotronic	*Pump Up the Jam*

MUSIC MANIA

Music enthusiasts live in interesting times. The variety of music available and the different ways to indulge their passion have never been greater. The advent of the computer has made accessibility and choice enormously easy for kids and adults.

The **Internet** may be the most significant advance. For those who have a computer and access to the Internet, some of the features it offers are:

- online shopping, often at good discounts and from an exhaustive catalogue. There are sites that specialize in obtaining rare recordings from almost every musical genre.

- several searchable databases. Is there a song you're trying to find but can't remember the name or the artist? Type in a part of a lyric and you'll likely turn up the one you're looking for.
- previews of new releases by your favorite artists.
- Web sites for various artists, which often have images, audio and video clips and personal info. Once in a while a performer may take part in an online "chat" session where fans can ask questions or make comments.

Computer software There are a number of types of computer software that are geared specifically to music. One of the most important advances to music and computers is MIDI (Musical Instrument Digital Interface). It is a standard that specifies how musical notes and other information are exchanged between electronic instruments and personal computers. The software involved in the system is called a MIDI sequencer. It enables, for example, a musician to play a composition on an electronic keyboard and have the composition recorded and stored digitally on a computer connected to the keyboard. The musician can then edit the music, change tempo, pitch, volume, or add other parts or tracks to the music. It is even possible to transpose a piece to a different key. The changes are limited only by the imagination. The composer can then print out a copy of the music created.

Other software programs are designed to aid composers. They allow you to type in the notes one by one and then play back the result. There are several of these available with varying degrees of complexity. Simple versions are available on the Internet as shareware.

Other programs available on compact discs and DVD contain biographical retrospectives of famous musicians such as Beethoven, Frank Sinatra or The Beatles. These are full multimedia presentations with video clips and audio accompaniment.

There are also custom databases that are programs specifically designed to keep track of your collections of sheet music, recorded music or videos.

The fast pace of innovation and change precludes mentioning any specific program but you can consult your local computer or software retailer for information on the type of program you want or search the Internet.

MOVIES ABOUT MUSIC

Music and movies go hand in hand and it is no secret that a good score can greatly enhance a movie. There are several wonderful films about music. Here are some suggestions:

Movies with musical themes

- *Amadeus* (1984) (PG) 158 min., F. Murray Abraham, Tom Hulce.
- *Beethoven Lives Upstairs* (1992) (G) Paul Soles, Sheila McCarthy, Fiona Reid.
- *Coal Miner's Daughter* (1980) (PG) 125 min., Sissy Spacek, Levon Helm.
- *Fantasia* (1940) (G) 120 min., Disney cartoon interpretation of various classical pieces.
- *Mr. Holland's Opus* (1995) (G) 143 min., Richard Dreyfuss, Olympia Dukakis.
- *Shine* (1997) (PG) 105 min., Geoffrey Rush.

Movie musicals

- *Grease* (1978) (PG) 110 min., Olivia Newton-John, John Travolta.
- *Mary Poppins* (1964) (G) 140 min., Julie Andrews, Dick van Dyke.
- *Oklahoma!* (1955) (G) 145 min., Shirley Jones, Rod Steiger, Eddie Albert.
- *The Sound of Music* (1965) (G) 174 min., Julie Andrews, Christopher Plummer.
- *The Wizard of Oz* (1939) (G) 101 min., Judy Garland, Jack Haley, Ray Bolger, Bert Lahr.
- *Tommy* (1975) (PG) 111 min., Oliver Reed, Roger Daltrey, Ann-Margret, Elton John.
- *West Side Story* (1961) (PG) 151 min., Natalie Wood, Richard Beymer.

Concert or biographical movies

- *Chuck Berry: Hail, Hail, Rock & Roll* (1987) (PG) 120 min., Chuck Berry & various artists.
- *Elvis* (1979) (PG) 150 min., Kurt Russell, made for TV autobiography of Elvis Presley.
- *Gimme Shelter* (1970) (PG) 91 min., documentary about the Rolling Stones.
- *That's Entertainment!* (1974) (G) 132 min., various stars.
- *The Compleat Beatles* (1982) (PG) 120 min.,- chronicle of the career of The Beatles.
- *Woodstock* (1970) (PG) 184 min., various artists documentary of the famous music festival.

Of particular note are a series of recordings and films based on stories by Susan Hammond that are excellent for kids:

- *Mr. Bach Comes to Call: A Tale of Enchantment*
- *Mozart's Magnificent Voyage*
- *Beethoven Lives Upstairs: A Tale of Childhood and Genius*
- *Tchaikovsky Discovers America*

These are all available on video cassette and may be available at the local library.

APPENDIX

Organizations

Here is a list of various organizations to contact for more information:

- *Canadian Music Educators Association*, 16 Royaleigh Ave., Etobicoke, Ont. M9P 2J5
- *Canadian Federation of Music Teachers Associations*, 812 Haig Rd., Ancaster, Ont. L9G 3G9
- *CAMMAC (Canadian Amateur Musicians/Musciens Amateurs du Canada)*, 4459 Sherbrooke St. W., Westmount, Que. H3Z 1L6
- *British Columbia Registered Music Teachers Association*, 914 Huntleigh Cr., Kamloops, B.C. V1S 1H1
- *Alberta Registered Music Teachers Association*, Percy Page Centre, 11759 Groat Rd., Edmonton, Alta. T5M 3K6
- *Saskatchewan Registered Music Teachers Association*, P.O. Box 120, Meacham, Sask. S0K 2V0
- *Manitoba Music Educators Association*, 191 Harcourt St., Winnipeg, Man. R3J 3H2
- *Ontario Registered Music Teachers Association*, P.O. Box 635, Timmins, Ont. P4N 7G2
- *Nova Scotia Music Educators Association*, 3106 Dutch Village Rd., Halifax, N.S. B3L 4L7
- *Newfoundland Registered Music Teachers Association*, 86 Old Topsall Rd., St. Johns, Nfld. A1C 2Z1
- *Kodály Society of Canada*, c/o Boosey and Hawkes, 279 Yorkdale Blvd., Willowdale, Ont. M2J 1S7

- *Music for Children, Carl Orff, Canada, Musique Pour Enfants*, 12 Meadow Cr., Guelph, Ont. N1H 6V2
- *Music for Young Children*, 72 Kingsford Ct., Kanata, Ont. K2K 1T9
- *Royal Conservatory of Music*, 273 Bloor St. W., Toronto, Ont. M5S 1W2
- *Kindermusik Canada Inc.*, P.O. Box 24152, Cambridge, Ont. N1R 8E7
- *Royal Canadian College of Organists*, 302-112 St. Clair Ave. W., Toronto, Ont. M4V 2Y3

OVER 100 CLASSIC COLES NOTES ARE ALSO AVAILABLE:

SHAKESPEARE

- Antony and Cleopatra
- Antony and Cleopatra Questions & Answers
- As You Like it
- Hamlet
- Hamlet in Everyday English
- Hamlet – Questions & Answers
- Julius Caesar
- Julius Caesar in Everyday English
- Julius Caesar Questions & Answers
- King Henry IV – Part 1
- King Henry V
- King Lear
- King Lear in Everyday English
- King Lear – Questions & Answers
- Macbeth
- Macbeth in Everyday English
- Macbeth – Questions & Answers
- Measure for Measure
- Merchant of Venice
- Merchant of Venice in Everyday English
- Merchant of Venice Questions & Answers
- Midsummer Night's Dream
- Midsummer Night's Dream in Everyday English
- Midsummer Night's Dream Questions & Answers
- Much Ado About Nothing
- Othello
- Othello in Everyday English
- Othello – Questions & Answers
- Richard II
- Richard III
- Romeo and Juliet
- Romeo and Juliet in Everyday English
- Romeo and Juliet Questions & Answers
- Taming of the Shrew
- Tempest
- Twelfth Night

SHAKESPEARE TOTAL STUDY ED

- Hamlet T.S.E.
- Julius Caesar T.S.E.
- King Henry IV – Part I T.S.E.
- King Lear T.S.E.
- Macbeth T.S.E.
- Merchant of Venice T.S.E.
- Othello T.S.E.
- Romeo and Juliet T.S.E.
- Taming of the Shrew T.S.E.
- Tempest T.S.E.
- Twelfth Night T.S.E.

LITERATURE AND POETRY

- Animal Farm
- Brave New World
- Catch 22
- Catcher in the Rye, Nine Stories
- Chrysalids, Day of the Triffids
- Crime and Punishment
- Crucible
- Death of a Salesman
- Diviners
- Duddy Kravitz and Other Works
- Edible Woman
- Emma
- Fahrenheit 451
- Farewell to Arms
- Fifth Business
- Glass Menagerie
- Grapes of Wrath
- Great Expectations
- Great Gatsby
- Gulliver's Travels
- Heart of Darkness
- Huckleberry Finn
- Ibsen's Works
- Iliad
- Jane Eyre
- King Oedipus, Oedipus at Colonus
- Lord of the Flies
- Lord of the Rings, Hobbit
- Man for All Seasons
- Mayor of Casterbridge
- 1984
- Odyssey
- Of Mice and Men
- Old Man and the Sea
- Oliver Twist
- One Flew Over the Cuckoos Nest
- Paradise Lost
- Pride and Prejudice
- Machiavelli's The Prince
- Pygmalion
- Scarlet Letter
- Separate Peace
- Sons and Lovers
- Stone Angel and Other Works
- Street Car Named Desire
- Surfacing
- Tale of Two Cities
- Tess of the D'Urbervilles
- To Kill a Mockingbird
- Two Solitudes
- Who Has Seen the Wind
- Wuthering Heights

Check the following stores:

CHAPTERS

COLES

SMITHBOOKS

WORLDS' BIGGEST BOOKSTORE

for our selection

THE CANTERBURY TALES

- The Canterbury Tales
- Prologue to the Canterbury Tales Total Study Edition
- Prologue to the Canterbury Tales

FRENCH

- French Grammar Questions & Answers
- French Grammar Simplified
- French Verbs Fully Conjugated
- French Verbs Simplified

CHEMISTRY

- Elementary Chemistry Notes Rev.
- How to Solve Chemistry Problems
- Introduction to Chemistry
- Senior Chemistry Notes Rev.

BIOLOGY

- Biology Notes

PHYSICS

- Elementary Physics Notes
- Senior Physics

MATHEMATICS

- Elementary Algebra Notes
- Secondary School Mathematics 1
- Secondary School Mathematics 4

REFERENCE

- Dictionary of Literary Terms
- Effective Term Papers and Reports
- English Grammar Simplified
- Handbook of English Grammar & Composition
- How to Write Good Essays & Critical Reviews
- Secrets of Studying English

For fifty years, Coles Notes have been helping students get through high school and university. New Coles Notes will help get you through the rest of life.

Look for these NEW COLES NOTES!

BUSINESS
- Effective Business Presentations
- Accounting for Small Business
- Write Effective Business Letters
- Write a Great Résumé
- Do A Great Job Interview
- Start Your Own Small Business
- Get Ahead at Work

PERSONAL FINANCE
- Basic Investing
- Investing in Stocks
- Investing in Mutual Funds
- Buying and Selling Your Home
- Plan Your Estate
- Develop a Personal Financial Plan

PARENTING
- Your Child: The First Year
- Your Child: The Terrific Twos
- Your Child: Ages Three and Four
- Raising A Reader
- Helping Your Child in Math
- Scholarships and Bursaries

SPORTS FOR KIDS
- Basketball for Kids
- Baseball for Kids
- Soccer for Kids
- Hockey for Kids
- Gymnastics for Kids
- Martial Arts for Kids

LIFESTYLE
- Wine
- Bartending
- Weddings
- Opera
- Casino Gambling
- Better Bridge
- Better Chess
- Better Tennis
- Better Golf
- Public Speaking
- Speed Reading
- Cooking 101
- Cats and Cat Care
- Dogs and Dog Care
- Wilderness Survival

PHRASE BOOKS
- French
- Spanish
- Italian
- German
- Russian
- Japanese
- Greek

GARDENING
- Indoor Gardening
- Perennial Gardening
- Herb Gardening
- Organic Gardening

Coles Notes and New Coles Notes are available at the following stores:
Chapters • Coles • Smithbooks • World's Biggest Bookstore

NOTES & UPDATES

NOTES & UPDATES

NOTES & UPDATES